Star Wars

US Tools of Space Supremacy

Loring Wirbel

Pluto Press

LONDON • STERLING, VIRGINIA

First published 2004 by Pluto Press
345 Archway Road, London N6 5AA
and 22883 Quicksilver Drive,
Sterling, VA 20166–2012, USA

www.plutobooks.com

British Library Cataloguing in Publication Data
A catalogue record for this book is available from the British Library

ISBN 0 7453 2115 1 hardback
ISBN 0 7453 2114 3 paperback

Library of Congress Cataloging in Publication Data
Wirbel, Loring, 1957–
  Star wars : US tools of space supremacy / Loring Wirbel.
     p. cm.
Includes bibliographical references and index.
  ISBN 0–7453–2115–1 (HARDBACK) — ISBN 0–7453–2114–3 (PAPERBACK)
  1. Ballistic missile defenses—United States. 2. Astronautics,
Military—United States. 3. Space weapons. 4. Space warfare. 5. Space
surveillance—United States. 6. Militarism—United States. 7. United
States—Military policy. 8. Military-industrial complex—United
States. I. Title.
  UG743.W56 2004
  358'.8'0973—dc22
                                                        2003015720

10   9   8   7   6   5   4   3   2   1

Designed and produced for Pluto Press by
Chase Publishing Services, Fortescue, Sidmouth, EX10 9QG, England
Typeset from disk by Stanford DTP Services, Northampton, England
Printed and bound in Canada by Transcontinental Printing

Contents

Acronyms and Abbreviations

ABL	Airborne Laser
ABM	Anti-Ballistic Missile
AFSA	Armed Forces Security Agency
AFSC	Air Force Space Command
ALCOR	ARPA-Lincoln (Labs) Coherent Observable Radar
ALTAIR	ARPA Long-Range Tracking And Instrumentation Radar
AMSTE	Affordable Moving Surface Target Engagement
ARPA	Advanced Research Projects Agency
ASAT	Anti-Satellite
AUV	Autonomous Underwater Vehicle
AWACS	Airborne Warning And Control System
BMDO	Ballistic Missile Defense Organization
BMEWS	Ballistic Missile Early Warning System
C4ISR	Command, Control, Communications, Computers, Intelligence, Surveillance, Reconnaissance
CALEA	Communication Assistance to Law Enforcement Act
CAOC	Combined Air Operations Center
CIA	Central Intelligence Agency
CMO	Central MASINT Office
COIL	Chemical Oxygen Iodine Laser
COMINT	Communications intelligence
CONAD	Continental Air Command
CPIS	Citizens for Peace In Space
CSOC	Consolidated Space Operations Center
DARO	Defense Airborne Reconnaissance Office
DARPA	Defense Advanced Research Projects Agency
DEFSMAC	Defense Special Misile And Aeronautics Center
DEW	Distant Early Warning radar system
DHS	Department of Homeland Security
DMSP	Defense Meteorological Satellite Program
DRAM	Dynamic Random Access Memory
DSCS	Defense Satellite Communication System
DSP	Defense Support Program
EELV	Evolved Expendable Launch Vehicle

ELINT	electronic intelligence
EMP	electro-magnetic pulse
EOKA	National Organization For Cypriot Struggle
EPLF	Ethiopian People's Liberation Front
ERIS	Exoatmospheric Re-Entry vehicle Interceptor Subsystem
ESA	European Space Agency
EXCOM	Executive Committee
FALCON	Force Application and Launch from Continental US
FAS	Federation Of American Scientists
FEWS	Follow-On Early Warning System
FIA	Future Imagery Architecture
FISC	Foreign Intelligence Surveillance Act
FIST	Fleet Imagery Support Terminal
FOL	Forward Operating Location
GBS	Global Broadcast System
GCHQ	Government Communications Headquarters
GPALS	Global Protection Against Limited Strikes
GPS	Global Positioning System
GRACE	Global Resource Action Center for the Environment
HAPDAR	Hard Point Demonstration Array Radar
HARM	High-Speed Anti-Radiation Missile
HEDI	High Endo-atmospheric Defense Interceptor
HUMINT	human intelligence
ICBM	intercontinental ballistic missile
ISA	Intelligence Support Activity
IUS	Inertial Upper Stage
JDAM	Joint Direct Attack Munition
JEDI	Joint Expeditionary Digital Information
Joint-STARS	Joint Surveillance Target Attack Reconnaissance System
KH	Keyhole
LEO	low-earth orbit
MAE	Metropolitan Area Exchange
MASINT	measurement and signature intelligence
MDA	Missile Defense Agency
MIDAS	Missile Defense Alarm System
MIRV	Multiple Independently-Targeted Re-Entry Vehicle
MOL	Manned Orbiting Laboratory
MONET	Multiple Wavelength Optical Network

MUOS	Mobile User Objective System
NACA	National Advisory Committee on Aeronautics
NADGE	NATO Air Defense Ground Environment
NAI	National Aerospace Initiative
NAP	Network Access Point
NASA	National Aeronautics and Space Administration
NATO	North Atlantic Treaty Organization
NGO	non-governmental organization
NIMA	National Imagery And Mapping Agency
NMD	National Missile Defense
NOAA	National Oceanic and Atmospheric Administration
NORAD	North American Air Defense Command
N-POESS	National Polar-Orbit Operational Environmental Satellite System
NPR	Nuclear Posture Review
NRO	National Reconnaissance Office
NSA	National Security Agency
NSC	National Security Council
ORS	Operationally Responsive Spacelift
OSR	Office Of Space Reconnaissance
PACBAR	Pacific Barrier Radar System
PAVE PAWS	PAVE = Air Force Program Name; Phased Array Warning System
PNAC	Project for a New American Century
PRESS	Pacific Range Electromagnetic Signature Study
QDR	Quadrennial Defense Review
RADINT	radar intelligence
RAF	Royal Air Force
RLV	Reusable Launch Vehicle
RMA	'revolution in military affairs'
RSOC	Regional SIGINT Operation Center
SAC	Strategic Air Command
SACEUR	Strategic Air Command Europe
SAGE	Semi-Automatic Ground Environment
SALT	Strategic Arms Limitation Treaty
SAMOS	Satellite and Missile Observation System
SBIRS	Space-Based Infrared System
SBL	Space-Based Laser
SBR	Space-Based Radar
SDI	Strategic Defense Initiative

SDIO	Strategic Defense Initiative Office
SDS	Satellite Data System
SIGINT	signals intelligence
SIPRNET	Secret IP Router Network
SLBM	submarine-launched ballistic missile
Sosus	sound surveillance system
STARS	Strategic Target System
START	Strategic Arms Reduction Talks
TCA	Transformational Communications Architecture
Tebac	Telemetry and Beacon Analysis Committee
TELINT	telemetry intelligence
TENCAP	Tactical Exploitation of National Capabilities
THAAD	Theater High Altitude Area Defense
TMD	theater missile defense
TSAT	Transformational Satellite
UAV	Unpiloted Aerial (Reconnaissance) Vehicle
UCAV	Unpiloted Combat Aerial Vehicle
UHF	ultra-high frequency
VHF	very high frequency
WebTAS	Web-enabled Timeline Analysis System
WGS	Wideband Gapfiller System
WWMCCS	Worldwide Military Command and Control System

Acknowledgements

My understanding of the way military space networks interoperate has been aided immensely by those scholars who make a point of sharing their work openly, including independent UK journalist Duncan Campbell, Jeffrey Richelson of National Security Archives, and John Pike of globalsecurity.org.

It is particularly gratifying to work with those arms researchers who combine study with action. I have been very lucky to have lived in the same community and shared many ideas with Bill Sulzman, director of Colorado-based Citizens for Peace in Space. Through Bill, I have met many brilliant members of the Global Network and War Resisters League affiliates, including Bruce Gagnon, Mary Beth Sullivan, Karl Grossman, Michio Kaku, Dave Webb, Regina Hagen, Stacey Fritz, Alice Slater, Sheila Baker, Peter Lumsdaine, Carol Rosin, David Knight of CND, and many other activists working in local communities. Frida Berrigan and William Hartung have assembled fine resources at the World Policy Institute, and through Frida and Bill Sulzman I have met many brilliant people associated with the Nukewatch community, including John LaForge, Bonnie Urfer, Jerry Berrigan, and Molly Mechtenberg-Berrigan.

My deepest respect goes to those who are willing to sacrifice personal freedoms to challenge space militarism: Lindis Percy and Anni Rainbow of the Campaign for the Accountability of American Bases; Helen John, Anne Lee, Wind Euler, and all the remarkable women of the WoMenwith Hill camp in Harrogate, UK; Sisters Carol Gilbert, Ardeth Platte, and Jackie Hudson of Jonah House; and of course, the many Colorado activists and members of CPIS, Pikes Peak Justice and Peace Commission, and Bijou Community, who are an endless source of inspiration on how to live one's beliefs.

To Carol and Abby
for their infinite patience and love

Preface

To many citizens concerned with matters of war and international relations, the notion of 'weapons in space' conjures futuristic images of laser battle-stations attacking other satellites in orbit around the Earth. Those familiar with the evolution of Star Wars missile-defense programs might also think of the kinetic-kill system, in which a small rocket slams into another rocket bearing a nuclear or chemical warhead – a system plagued by far more failures than successes in its development. Neither type of weapon has been perfected.

This book will argue, however, that space weapons exist today. They have been successfully deployed and used in Afghanistan and Iraq, solely for the benefit of the US, the UK, and the restricted 'coalition of concern' willing to accept the new notion of international unilateralism promoted by the US.

When a precision bomb is dropped on Tikrit, guided to its target by Global Positioning System satellites, a space weapon has been used. When an unmanned aerial 'robot' plane fires a missile at a car full of suspected al-Qaeda operatives in Yemen, using electronic intelligence to confirm its target, a space weapon has been used. US military leaders are united in their agreement that an evolution implemented through battlefields in Kosovo, Afghanistan and Iraq has perfected the notion of space-based warfare. Yet few citizens worldwide recognize this role of space as 'the force multiplier for full-spectrum dominance extending from sensor to shooter,' as it is touted in the Pentagon.

Such overwhelming capabilities would be worthy of critical concern if they were exploited equally by NATO, the Russian Federation, and China. But when combined with the new unilateralism spelled out in the pre-emptive doctrine employed by the Bush administration since early 2002, space-based military superiority represents an international crisis of the first order. The danger lies not only in using space to implement the type of unilateralism exercised in the attack on Iraq. Military space advocates also talk openly of space 'negation' – denying the use of orbital space not merely to adversaries at times of crisis, but even to close allies if the use of space interferes with US space dominance. This policy of negation is a primary reason the US Defense Department has tried to stop the European Space Agency from going ahead with plans for its own navigational satellite system, the Galileo network.

Diplomats and activists anxious to prevent the extension of pre-emptivity to new targets within the current 'axis of evil' need to make space a primary venue of their focus. The danger of unchallenged empire is serious when conventional weapons are used, but this is not the end of the story. In the latter half of this decade, new roles for nuclear weapons will be added to this heady mix.

The original conservative coalition promoting a 'revolution in military affairs' (RMA) talked of precision weapons and instant intelligence as a power that made nuclear weapons unnecessary. This is not what the Bush administration has in mind. Since its promulgation of the Nuclear Posture Review in early 2002, the Defense Department under Donald Rumsfeld has made clear that it wants to rely on nuclear weapons as another arrow in the quiver of space dominance, used alongside precision conventional weapons and total intelligence dominance to better control nations in the developing world that might get out of line. Of course, this makes the flap over weapons of mass destruction sound hypocritical in the extreme, but this is of no concern to the US Defense Department. The US will constantly insist on the right to military tools it will deny to all other nations worldwide.

This policy, set forth in new weapons development efforts, was codified in a meeting held at Strategic Command headquarters in Nebraska in August 2003. Military space experts got together with nuclear planners for the first time since the US victory in Iraq. The US Air Force Space Command had proposed a new program at the time of the Iraq invasion, called 'Operationally Responsive Spacelift' (ORS), which would solidify the dominance of near-Earth space that had been demonstrated so conclusively in the attack on Iraq. ORS called for moving well beyond NASA's civilian program for an Orbital Space Plane to replace the Space Shuttle, instead promoting a massive-lift space plane which could serve as an instant-launch attack or reconnaissance vehicle, as well as a platform for carrying heavy satellites into orbit.

The ORS program also proposed moving the kinetic-kill vehicles used in missile-defense programs, directly into orbiting satellites. This way, missiles from adversary states could be attacked in early launch phases, before multiple warheads separated from their launch vehicles. The potential for such space-borne kinetic-kill vehicles to violate the Outer Space Treaty of 1967 did not seem to be a concern for Pentagon planners.

There was much more under consideration at the August meeting: a new reserve force of Minuteman-III intercontinental missiles was touted, one that would be used for fast launches of either precision conventional weapons or nuclear weapons, with little concern over how ICBM missile counts of such dual-purpose rockets would be handled under existing treaties. Planning would begin for a next generation of intercontinental missile, Minuteman-IV, which might return to the mobile basing of the original MX missile, and might also be armed with new earth-penetrating nuclear warheads designed at Los Alamos National Labs. Pop-up surveillance or missile-defense satellites might now be launched within hours of a decision to deploy, taken to space by a mix of expendable launch vehicles, space planes, and even fighter-jets configured to handle satellite launches. All space-based and high-altitude atmospheric military programs, and all programs designed for intelligence, space warfare, or missile-defense duties, would now come under common management, serving the new US goal of pre-emptive attack on other nations, and absolute dominance of orbital space.

The familiar 'Star Wars' missile-defense weapons, when combined with the precision navigation, intelligence, targeting, and communication tools in space used to such an effect in Iraq, no longer can be seen as protective Maginot lines in space or on the ground, used to guard against rogue states with intermediate weapons. In fact, the entire purpose of multi-tiered missile defense is shifted to making pre-emptive space dominance more effective for the US and those nations deemed its friends.

How had the US military achieved such overwhelming capabilities, combined with frightening doctrines on weapon use, in the two short years since the September 11 attacks? The easy answer would point to the explicit empire-building doctrines favored by Rumsfeld and key Defense Department underlings like Richard Perle and Paul Wolfowitz. But relying on the short-term promulgation of explicit superiority theories would minimize the evolution of space superiority tools developed over the past 50 years, and honed with particular speed since the demise of the Soviet Union in 1991. To understand how the US government came to believe that space was its own playground, this book will examine the roots of technologies and policies present for decades, coming to a head under the tutelage of the new empire-builders of the Bush administration. It will explore the expansion of electronic intelligence under Presidents Truman and Eisenhower, the initiation of crude space defense and intelligence tools under Kennedy and Johnson, and the move to coordinate military space networks under Nixon, Ford, and Carter. Ronald Reagan's Star Wars visions of the 1980s become less of an anomaly, and more of an integrated part of a unilateral military build-up that expanded through the era of George Bush the Elder, when military spending by the Soviet Union began its precipitous decline.

This book casts particular blame on the two-term period of Bill Clinton, despite the fact that Clinton is excoriated by missile-defense advocates for 'disarming America.' In reality, Clinton deliberately ignored opportunities to limit global weapons and intelligence networks as the Soviet Union collapsed, and the successor Russian space networks deteriorated. After a brief dalliance with multilateral military missions, Clinton became a strong proponent of unilateral action, as expressed by his second Secretary of State, Madeleine Albright. Clinton encouraged officials from the National Reconnaissance Office, the nation's largest intelligence agency, and the US Space Command, to promulgate doctrines and make speeches insisting on a sole right to control space.

By the time George Bush arrived in office, space unilateralism already was assumed to be the way the world worked. Long before Donald Rumsfeld and Peter Teets, the director of the National Reconnaissance Office under Bush, were waxing about the 'transformational' power of merging Defense Department, NRO, NASA, and Missile Defense Agency assets, the US Space Command had prepared the path for global domination with its *Vision for 2020* document of 1996, setting out the requirement that the US control the planet by single-handedly controlling space. The unilateral empire-building that at first blush seemed unique to the younger George Bush had, in reality, been set in motion through the administrations of both his father and the two-term Democratic administration of Bill Clinton.

*   *   *

Still, neither the Iraq war opponents nor the peace-in-space activists had cast their vision back far enough in time to grasp the roots of unilateral space militarism, nor had they broadened their view to see intelligence, communications, and missile defense as parts of one whole.

Unilateralism, of course, could only be perfected following the demise of the Soviet Union. But asymmetry in global networks was built into superpower confrontations well before World War II came to an end. When Marxists claimed that the Yalta conference had been rigged from the beginning for Roosevelt and Churchill to take advantage of Stalin, there were germs of truth in their complaints. While few can deny the expansionist and totalitarian aims of Stalin in the post-war period, the assumptions driving the Yalta partitioning were that Western allied forces would be the primary controllers of air and sea lanes in the period of reconstruction following the war, as well as of space lanes of the future. The Soviet Union would be allocated an acceptable buffer region, but should not expect to extend its control of the Black Sea and northern Arctic approaches to any projection of sea power.

When Churchill and Roosevelt signed the secret BRUSA Treaty in 1943, followed by an expanded five-nation UKUSA Treaty in 1947, this asymmetry was codified in the first global technology domain that mattered for military power projection – signals intelligence. Electronic intelligence carried out on the closed societies of the socialist nations would be handled by a tight team of intelligence officials in the five leading Caucasian, English-speaking nations: the US, the UK, Canada, Australia, and New Zealand. The UKUSA Treaty set the template for all such tiered relationships that were later established for air and space control. Even though UKUSA in its early years relied on ground-based antenna farms and primitive airborne reconnaissance platforms, it assumed the existence of a global network of electronic information managed by allied powers, a model that could be applied perfectly to space control.

The first computerized air-defense networks were designed in the early 1950s, even as the US and the UK were establishing global bases for forward projection of nuclear fission weapons, and perfecting delivery systems for much larger fusion weapons. Electronic intelligence bases often were co-located with nuclear weapons bases, or served as enablers for nuclear attack, though their heavy secrecy prevented any activists in the nascent ban-the-bomb movement from making the connection between nuclear weapons and electronic intelligence.

Air defense networks, and the radar chains that served as homeland intelligence first-responders, were sold through the same fear factors that later served Ronald Reagan in touting missile defense. The natural secrecy of the Soviet Union, combined with Nikita Khrushchev's tendency to exaggerate technology accomplishments, made it easy for American and NATO officials to frighten the citizens of allied nations into approving global expansion of air intelligence. Yet the occasional honesty of internal policy leaders like George Kennan made it clear that Truman and Eisenhower shared a desire to frighten the population into higher defense spending, using skewed analyses of technical capabilities that deliberately hid the asymmetric assumptions that defined how US and western European defense officials viewed the bipolar world.

When the newly-socialist China went nuclear with the help of the Soviet Union, Gen. Curtis LeMay and others in the Pentagon advocated first-strike attacks on China's Lop Nor nuclear facilities. Eisenhower ruled out pre-emptive warfare as a matter of principle, yet was willing to consider tactical nuclear strikes when he perceived a region as falling under communist influence, as he did in Vietnam in 1954. Obviously, the under-mining of smaller states through covert means was seen as a preferable, even ethical, way of expanding influence during the Cold War, a low-key alternative to making the type of nuclear threats tacitly made in Indochina.

The race to exploit space in the decade following the launch of Sputnik represented the only era where military space advocates could claim a defensive role in building up satellite networks. The policies of US civilian leaders reflected a genuine shock among US citizens that the Soviet Union had managed to move so far ahead in satellite technology, a shock amplified by the string of successes the Soviet space program witnessed after Sputnik, and the equal number of failures experienced by the Discoverer program. Because conservatives in the US Congress were gaining mileage with fears of bomber gaps and missile gaps, the developers of spy satellites could honestly claim to be taking the liberal position of using space technology on a closed society to disprove claims of massive arms superiority, thereby cutting the need for the US government to escalate the arms race further.

From the beginning, however, the valiant civilian space race always was a bit of a scam. Several authors of NASA histories have pointed out how the race to the moon was conducted primarily, if not solely, for propaganda purposes, particularly by John F. Kennedy, who wanted a way to cool Khrushchev's nasty rhetoric. Thanks to declassification in the mid-1990s at the National Reconnaissance Office, the nation's primary space intelligence agency, we learned that the entire Discoverer satellite program was a cover for Corona, the country's first generation of covert imaging satellites. Less commonly known is that many of the key scientists identified as initiators of the Gemini and Apollo programs at NASA, including Brockway McMillan, Alexander Flax, and Hans Mark, were also directors of the NRO. Throughout the history of NASA, space assets were intended for intelligence and military communications first, and civilian missions a distant second. The practical effect of the NRO's ties to arms-site inspections from space was that, as arms negotiators began working on the Anti-Ballistic Missile and Strategic Arms Limitation Treaties, space-based intelligence was assumed to be the source of stability in international relations. Because no one in traditional arms-control communities questioned the direction or intent of 'national technical means of verification,' they learned to simply keep their mouths shut.

During the 1960s, terrestrial radar programs were upgraded for three purposes, kept carefully segmented for public consumption. Small tracking and acquisition radars were developed for the new Sentinel and Safeguard anti-ballistic missile programs, aimed at the ambitious but largely unachievable mission of taking out a missile in flight. Larger search radar, both traditional systems such as BMEWS and electrically-steerable phased arrays such as Pave

Paws, were deployed worldwide to provide as early a warning as possible of a Soviet missile attack (though with no launch-on-warning program in US Strategic Air Command, the utility of the information was questionable). Finally, highly secret radar systems were installed by the National Security Agency in locations such as Turkey and Iran, to give more detailed information on Soviet space testing facilities. Behind the scenes, Pentagon officials admitted the distinctions between missile defense and intelligence had been artificial ones from the beginning.

Between the Nixon and Reagan administrations, complex imaging and signals intelligence satellites were developed and launched, giving the US the ability to see and hear everything going on worldwide on a 24-hour basis. Because US aerospace contractors and civilian semiconductor companies were far ahead of Soviet state agencies in designing microelectronic subsystems, the Soviet Cosmos series of satellites fell further and further behind American counterparts. The ability of the new US satellites to report their information in real-time, without significant delay, made their intelligence take more interesting to tactical battle commanders in the field. But the new satellites also required specialized large ground stations, which became the target of localized protests around the world, adding to the general challenge of US interests that took place in developing nations in the late 1970s.

Ronald Reagan remains the only US president to promote missile defense under a genuine belief that the technology of space-based directed-energy weapons and ground-based kinetic destruction weapons would truly be used to protect US populations. In private, Defense Secretary Caspar Weinberger and other DoD officials intimated to allies and contractors that Reagan's March 1983 speech really was about protecting first-strike weapons, in order to better carry out attacks on others. The centerpiece weapons for the Strategic Defense Initiative, in particular the space-based X-ray laser, were pipe dreams promoted by Edward Teller and associates. The Reagan cabinet members realized this all the time, but promoted SDI for its war-fighting capabilities. It remains an open question the degree to which Reagan comprehended the limitations, and outright misuses, of his dream of absolute defense. The one useful legacy of the Reagan years was that many of the same British citizens opposed to new European tactical nuclear weapons became opponents of Star Wars, and of the massive expansion of space intelligence at Menwith Hill, Bude, and other UK bases.

In the US, coordinated anti-nuclear activity did not survive the eased tensions of the Gorbachev years. Perhaps as important, the anti-SDI and anti-nuclear activists that continued to monitor the Bush–Gorbachev START treaties did not find common cause with civil liberties activists expressing growing concern about global snooping programs such as Echelon. In fact, with arms-control centrists taking center stage as START cheerleaders, the old habit of believing the NRO and the NSA could do no wrong retained its power through the late Bush and early Clinton years. As a result, no one questioned intelligence budgets spiraling beyond $5 billion per agency per year. Consequently, Weinberger was able to continue to promote missile-defense weapons in the first Bush administration, touting the same weapons (minus the X-ray laser) for tactical purposes against smaller rogue nations, that had been promoted for direct challenges to the Soviet Union only months before.

The bipartisan support in the US for maintaining and expanding existing military bases, even in the face of the Soviet Union's dissolution, assured that any talk of a 'peace dividend' under the new Clinton administration remained a pipe dream. In fact, after a brief dalliance with multilateralism, Clinton became a firm advocate of a resurgent US military, particularly one that carried out missions unilaterally. After Bush the Elder declassified the NRO in his final months in office, the agency made a point of launching programs to better disseminate its intelligence product to military agencies in regional fields. Clinton, meanwhile, oversaw an expansion of the US Space Command and its mission of using space assets, particularly intelligence assets, in order to control all planetary resources through space. This strategy was spelled out explicitly in the US Space Command's 1996 *Vision for 2020* document.

The same Bill Clinton that was denounced by conservatives for alleged opposition to missile defense, actually held a steady line on basic Star Wars research, while vastly expanding the use and application of space intelligence products. Jeff Harris and Keith Hall, directors of the NRO during the Clinton years, began talking explicitly in public about the virtues of space dominance.

Only a valiant few public-interest organizations made the necessary connections of all these programs during the Clinton years, including Citizens for Peace in Space, Global Network Against Weapons and Nuclear Power in Space, the Center for Defense Information, the Western States Legal Foundation, and the British Campaign for Nuclear Disarmament. Many NGOs and citizen lobbies during the Clinton years heard and saw, but refused to believe.

The reticence changed when George W. Bush came to office on the heels of a report from a national commission, headed by Donald Rumsfeld, warning of a 'space Pearl Harbor' if the US did not dominate space in an absolute sense. Even prior to the al-Qaeda attacks of September 11, 2001, activists were alarmed by the administration's announced intentions to renounce the ABM Treaty, and to act against the European Space Agency's attempts to develop an independent space navigational network.

Since the heavy use of space assets in Afghanistan and Iraq served as proof to military commanders of the value in merging intelligence, communications, and precision-weapons assets, notions of pre-emptive space warfare have become common-place. The right of pre-emptive planetary management is now virtually assumed by all Bush administration officials, with the operational success silencing any ethical questions involved in telling other nations what to do. In fact, military officers formerly within the intelligence establishment or regional commands have been more likely in recent months to warn of the limits of space pre-emptivity than have civilian politicians in executive or legislative branches.

Adding nuclear weapons to this volatile mix constituted the strategists' *coup de grâce*, and was easy to anticipate after the US Space Command and Strategic Command were merged in October 2002. All that was necessary was a strategic vision to unite the prospects for next-generation nuclear weapons, with the extant plans for conducting war in and from space. The August meeting in Nebraska represented the first step in making this vision concrete.

The ramifications of melding doctrines of pre-emptivity and space dominance are profound and multi-faceted. Not only do they represent a travesty for foreign policy visions that emphasize a multilateral UN, but there are civil liberties concerns (already recognized by the anti-Echelon community) of exploiting space-based intelligence tools across the NRO, the NSA, Northern Command, and the Department of Homeland Security. The unilateralists in the Bush administration have made clear their plans for conducting war around the globe using the medium of space. It is high time the anti-nuclear, global justice, civil liberties, anti-BMD, and anti-war communities catch up with these plans by uniting their own efforts at exposing and opposing the space domination.

Introduction

For more than 40 years, students of both nuclear deterrence theory and of anti-missile technology development have analyzed the birth, development, and demise of the Anti-Ballistic Missile (ABM) Treaty with only minimal consideration of the wider policies of militarizing space. By adopting such a restrictive viewpoint, friends and foes alike of ABM take as a given the assumption that the purpose of Star Wars weapons truly is defensive, intended to knock out errant missiles from so-called rogue states.

This certainly was not the case when defensive weapons were debated seriously for the first time in the Lyndon Johnson administration, during the height of the Cold War. The very concept that US Defense Secretary Robert McNamara found hardest to sell to Soviet Ambassador Alexei Kosygin in 1967 was that of defensive weapons allowing and encouraging a first-strike offensive posture.[1] It took the five years between US promotion of the Sentinel ABM program in 1967 and the signing of the ABM Treaty in 1972, for US and Soviet strategists to realize that an effective defensive weapon allowed for a more comprehensive 'breakout' into a first-strike advantage, in the event of nuclear hostilities, than might otherwise be possible. ABM weapons could enable a first-strike total dominance by a nation that chose to use its nuclear weapons first, with anti-missile weapons held as a hedge.

Of course, what was true in a finely-balanced bipolar world applied even more directly when the United States became a unilateral hyperpower, following the demise of the Soviet Union. Ronald Reagan gave analysts a foretaste of what the new justification for Star Wars might look like, when he promoted space-based weapons in 1983 under the mantra of providing Americans with the perfect security umbrella. Because nuclear deterrence policy still stood in the 1980s in somewhat tattered form, the criticisms of Reagan's provocative military policies did not extend to a wider recognition of the Strategic Defense Initiative (SDI) as the enabler of a first-strike policy. Instead, Star

Wars critics were content to warn that ground-based missile interceptors could always be overwhelmed by countermeasures, and that an H-bomb-pumped X-ray laser in space was an unrealizable dream promoted by Edward Teller.

As the unilateralists come out of the closet 20 years later, making clear their desire for global domination, some in the arms-control community believe that the application of Star Wars as a tool for empire expansion began with the rise to power of the Rumsfeld–Wolfowitz–Perle clique within the current Bush administration. Other missile-defense analysts still refuse to recognize even this much, considering the programs of the Missile Defense Agency (MDA) as separate and unrelated elements to the world-dominating dogma laid out in the Bush administration's September 2002 guidebook for global control, *National Security Strategy of the United States*.[2] But what the Bush team has done in the aftermath of the September 11 attacks is merely make explicit, with a certain amount of pride, what the Clinton administration had been preparing in a tacit sense since the end of the Cold War.

The full extent of space military policy cannot be grasped without considering the changed missions for space-based intelligence, communications, navigation, and targeting in the last decade. The multi-billion dollar network designed to monitor the Soviet Union and China during the Cold War was talked about as little as possible during the days of bipolar rivalry, and hence left unexamined as the first Bush administration provided new negotiating possibilities to the incoming Clinton administration. Since Soviet strategic nuclear networks, as well as the communications and intelligence networks supporting them, were falling into disrepair as the Soviet empire shrunk back to its Russian roots, the time was ripe for careful pruning of space-based military networks fielded by the US, or at least a restructuring of such networks for shared multilateral goals.

But the Somalia and Rwanda debacles left the Clinton administration with little reason to support multilateralism. Hence, it was easy for warfighter advocates within the military to promote the direct re-purposing of existing space-based networks to the mission of enabling first-strike warfare, ranging from the smallest of regional battles to the familiar '2½ War' scenarios of the Pentagon.[3] When CIA Director James Woolsey warned in 1993 that the Soviet dragon had been slain but that many snakes remained in the garden, Pentagon representatives from the Space Command, the National Reconnaissance Office (NRO), and the National Security Agency (NSA) took the speech as a sign that Cold War space networks could be upgraded and expanded to go after any snake deemed appropriate.

At first blush, such actions could seem defensive and prescient, particularly when coupled with the global concern over weapons of mass destruction in the hands of states or actors deemed unstable. But rhetoric indicated a different goal. Beginning early in the Clinton administration, Space Command and the NRO (whose mission and existence had been declassified only in the waning days of the Bush administration, despite having been conceived in 1960) went public with very explicit statements, indicating that the goal of space-based military networks was no longer verification of arms treaties, but provision of real-time information to enable first-strike victories in any venue worldwide. Clinton administration insiders at first tried to suggest that this was loose Pentagon talk, unsupported by the civilian voices within the State Department, but Madeleine Albright's increasing support of unilateralism during the second Clinton term made clear that global dominance was fully supported by the civilian leadership.

The problem, as arms analysts Michael Klare and William Arkin have pointed out several times in the past decade, is that tacit world domination is a goal that most politicians in both major US parties supported in theory, but never wished to talk about. Since September 11, of course, unapologetic triumphalist imperialism is now an acceptable philosophy across the mainstream political spectrum, allowing observers from Thomas Friedman to Sebastian Mallaby to suggest that the more US leaders assume the jodhpurs and pith helmets of the British colonialist era, the safer the world will be from terrorists and rogue states. But in the 1990s, 'full-spectrum dominance' was touted only by the space forces within the military, while civilian political leaders winked, nodded, and shoveled money in the appropriate direction.

The unity of domination goals was not as explicit as conspiracy theorists would wish to believe. Clinton's Ballistic Missile Defense Organization did not conduct regular meetings with those in

Space Command and the NRO who talked of using intelligence to provide the ultimate asymmetric advantage in battle. Missile-defense specialists certainly did not advise the NSA and the NRO on the turn to space for the bulk of upgraded elements in the global Echelon spy network. But the commonality of interests fed policies of domination. Schriever Air Force Base in Colorado, for example, was the central control location for major navigational, targeting, and communication satellites. It was also the home of the Space Warfare Center and the Joint National Integration Facility, a center for simulating missile-defense encounters. And it was the headquarters for the Talon missions and Project Strike, mid-1990s experiments that used space networks to provide 'real-time intelligence to the warfighter.' Is it any wonder that these disparate threads of space military policy fed the common goal of unilateral US control of the planet by the midpoint of the George W. Bush administration?

Failure to consider the role played by existing space networks in support of pre-emptive warfare does more than provide an incomplete analysis of missile-defense weapons. It leads many arms-control advocates to press for the worthwhile but incomplete goal of halting *weaponization* of space, without considering how space-based non-weaponized military networks serve as enablers of pre-emptive, and even preventive, warfare. Arms-control traditionalists certainly are correct in assuming that near-Earth space can never return to Antarctica-like status, as the Outer Space Treaty of 1967 envisioned space to be. Because no nation, in the 36 years since the treaty was signed, was willing to challenge the overall purpose served by a specific space-based network, systems that constituted first-strike weapons in all but name were allowed in space through tacit agreement. Just because the actual weapon resides on the ground or in the atmosphere does not mean that the overall weapon system based in space is not just as destabilizing as a space-based laser.

Unfortunately, sober analysis of such systems would have required arms-control advocates to carefully study the technical capabilities of multiple systems, many of which were classified, while determining how those systems applied to the announced war-fighting strategies of the nation. They were scarcely up to the task. In a 2003 study for *Bulletin of the Atomic Scientists*, Michael Krepon of the Henry L. Stimson Center divided national security specialists into 'dominators' and 'conciliators.' He suggested that the dominators so utterly defined security policy in the Bush administration, the conciliators were unable to come up with rational arguments for multilateralism.[4]

But these conciliators clearly had been asleep at the switch during the Clinton administration. Just as Clinton killed off the Kyoto environmental treaty in all but name in 1999, leaving Bush to renounce it explicitly when in office, Clinton had encouraged the rise of space-domination advocates who made their arguments for total planetary control in very public forums, yet without a counter-argument from those whom Krepon calls the conciliators. Now, not only would it be a bit late for the conciliators to attempt to put limits on Bush's naked imperialism strategy, but who among the nascent ABM Treaty proponents would be up to the task of determining when a space navigational system like the Global Positioning System became destabilizing when supporting a strategy like 'NavWar'?

Truth be told, conciliators historically have not wanted to examine technology too closely. During the early years of arms negotiations, space-based systems constituted the 'national technical means of verification,' which could not be discussed openly, at the risk of upsetting the SALT (Strategic Arms Limitation Treaty) apple cart. Many arms-control advocates still retain the mistaken belief that everything the NSA and NRO do is stabilizing by nature. The conscious decision to maintain ignorance left conciliators unprepared to address the change in mission of the technical intelligence and communications agencies.

A handful of analysts have warned since the Carter era that a combined analysis of space 'C4ISR' (Command, Control, Communications, Computers, Intelligence, Surveillance, Reconnaissance) and advanced nuclear and missile-defense strategies would be critical in the twenty-first century. Desmond Ball, a respected Australian specialist on nuclear war-fighting strategies, published a book in 1980 on the Pine Gap intelligence base in Australia, *A Suitable Piece of Real Estate*, in which he argued that precision and real-time distribution in intelligence networks was as dangerous as precision in missile warhead accuracy. British intelligence analyst Duncan Campbell and New Zealand writer and activist Nicky Hager similarly have tied together the plans for intelligence expansion and for Star Wars.[5]

Comprehension of the evolution of technical intelligence agencies in the United States has been aided by excellent analyses from independent authors and researchers such as James Bamford, John Pike, and Jeffrey Richelson. Too often, however, researchers can fall victim to the same 'Beltway disease' that affects all too many US-based non-governmental organizations – the longer an interest group stays in Washington, the more its viewpoints take into account those of the powerful. This is aided by the fact that the friendliest voices in Congress, outside of a few ultra-conservative members reflexively suspicious of intelligence agencies, adopt a position on the hawkish side of a mild conciliator.

Except for occasional thoughtful efforts from independent members of Congress like Representative Dennis Kucinich, policy-makers in Washington are either adamantly in favor of US policies of global dominance, or tacitly accepting of systems that enable such dominance to take place. Krepon, for example, suggested that conciliators would be well-advised to accept a ground-based layer of terminal-phase missile-defense weapons in order to forestall more expansive systems in the future. He also suggested that prevention of weaponization of space may require that conciliators accept military networks in space that enable first-strike warfare.

This book will argue that these incremental conciliator steps might be necessary for a first-pass effort to challenge the dominators, but are scarcely sufficient in developing long-term strategies based on coalitions of nations and multilateral military efforts. Tactical deals allowing limited kinetic-kill missile-defense weapons,[6] or region-specific theater missile defense, will serve only to encourage regional or technology-specific arms races, while failing to whet the appetites of the missile-defense proponents. Proposals that draw the line at weapons in space will allow for the continued existence of first-strike weapon systems which have primary non-weapon elements dwelling in space.

This book proposes a return to the ideals of the 1967 Outer Space Treaty. Near-Earth space is not the sole venue of the US military, and the United States should be forbidden through international law from adopting any doctrines advocating unilateral use. Military networks may always be resident in space, but should be monitored by an international agency similar to the Missile Technology Control Regime, to prevent the kind of 'technological creep' that leads to in-orbit systems attaining the capability to support pre-emptive warfare. No nation should be barred from orbiting satellites, but all nations should be excluded from launching either anti-satellite weapons, or space weapons supporting missile-defense missions. Missile defense itself, since it is closer to supporting first-strike unilateralist philosophies than it was in the days of Sentinel and Safeguard, should be banned worldwide as a destabilizing arms technology. Strategies of any nation that propose using space, sea, or air lanes to achieve total dominance over land or resources outside that nation's boundaries, should be prohibited under international law. These goals seem at once too radical to even consider in the twenty-first-century environment, and also a natural extension of the principles under which the United Nations was founded following World War II. This only shows how far the world has gone in accepting US unilateralism.

Passing off the dirty work on the planet to a superpower that claims unfair rights often represents the easiest way for less powerful nations to solve problems. But such a 'planetary consensus,' evidenced at times in the buildup to war in Iraq, cannot be seen as a healthy international environment. True multilateralism is a far more difficult and messy way to organize affairs, both on Earth and in space. But those who choose the simpler path should beware the old adage, 'Be careful what you wish for.'

1

The Birth of Intelligence Policy and Space Use

Before rocketry had captured the imagination of either civilian scientists or military leaders as a near-term reality for space exploration or warfare, before nuclear weapons had graduated from one-time exemplar of terror to a regular tool of superpower leverage, signals intelligence already had demonstrated its utility to a small, tightly-knit cabal within the victorious allied powers. The number of people that understood the way that interception of radio traffic and cracking complex military codes interleaved in the new complex science of cryptography and signals intelligence, were numbered in the low hundreds at the end of World War II. Yet cryptography's importance was obvious to those in the know. The cracking of the Soviet Venona one-time-pad codes[1] at the end of World War II allowed the United States to verify the existence and identity of Soviet spies operating within the US, and proved the utility of the Signal Security Agency and its successor, the Armed Forces Security Agency (AFSA). It took the temporary defeat of US forces on the Korean peninsula in 1950 to finally turn the small US signals intelligence community into a globe-circling network, but the elements of a listening web surrounding the Soviet Union were in place by mid-1945.

During both world wars, signals intelligence was merely an enabling activity for codebreaking, and the standard of excellence was set by the British cryptographers at Bletchley Park, who cracked the German Enigma machine. The main task for interception teams was to determine the relevant radio frequencies used by adversary military agencies, and to attempt to tap into land lines when possible, particularly at aggregation points, such as submarine cable landing points and telephone switching centers, where scores of individual circuit-switched calls were multiplexed.

Those engineers involved in basic research in antenna and sensor design were aware that signals intelligence could include the interception of any emanation across the electromagnetic spectrum. Traditionally, however, researchers in British air-defense fields working on radar technology were segregated from radio interception specialists. As the technology for manufacturing key electronic items such as klystron power tubes moved to the US, however, American defense contractors realized the common technology base spanning radar and electronic intelligence platforms. As allied intelligence groups scoured for hints of Soviet intentions at the end of World War II, the unified nature of electronic intelligence was recognized by many theorists and practical engineers.

Imaging intelligence, including both visible light and infrared imaging, almost always is managed separately from all other electromagnetic interception, since it evolved from overhead aerial reconnaissance, and only belatedly was dependent on advances in photo processing, electronic image capture, and 'hyperspectral' analysis covering several frequency bands. Through the Cold War, imaging was handled by the CIA's National Photographic Interpretation Center, and later by the National Imagery and Mapping Agency (NIMA), only coming together with signals information at the level of the space-based intelligence agency, the National Reconnaissance Office.

Signals intelligence, or SIGINT, includes both communications and electronic intelligence. Communications intelligence, or COMINT, traditionally refers to intercepted messages generated by any communications or computer platform generating a linear message intended to be interpreted by humans. Electronic intelligence, or ELINT, involves the study of emanations of radar, electronic systems in planes and ships, and the like. Later in the Cold War, telemetry intelligence (TELINT) and measurement and signature intelligence (MASINT) were added to the roster, respectively referring to the interception of data automatically generated by missiles in flight, and data collected from nuclear bomb tests, chemical emissions, and similar non-electromagnetic sources. The latter intelligence was often gathered by specialty military organizations like the Air Force Technical Applications Center, and is currently the responsibility within the Pentagon of the Central MASINT Office, or CMO.

While comprehension of the unity of technical intelligence was still piecemeal in 1945, the drive for establishing global listening webs was apparent virtually from the day of German defeat. The tedious Marxist claims that the Cold War was born in a Western race for empire sounded hollow to those on the front lines of Eastern Europe at the end of World War II, observing the Soviet putsches that established vassal states in mixed-economy nations like Poland and Czechoslovakia. Yet the assumptions of how the world was to be parceled up by Western powers always bore a whiff of empire building, particularly in the establishment of 'white boys' clubs' meant to delineate global spoils for industrial nations.

The United States and Britain were the only two allied nations with significant signals intelligence and cryptography expertise at the end of the war – the US provided funding and technology for building global networks, while British crypto and radar expertise developed at wartime labs was widely appreciated in US scientific circles. When the United States and Britain established the BRUSA Pact for cryptography and radio-interception sharing in 1943, predecessor to the wider UKUSA Treaty of 1947, there never was a thought given to including the Soviet Union on signals intelligence discussions. The so-called even balance of the Cold War was predicated upon a version of containment: the Soviet Union was allowed free rein to implement policies in its own periphery and that of Eastern Europe (later extended to China), but open seas and air lanes belonged primarily to Western allies.

As 'mass retaliation' weapons evolved from B-29-based A-bombs to B-52 H-bombs, and finally to land- and sea-based missiles, the underlying assumption of Cold War boundaries rested upon a boxed-in Soviet alliance and a free-ranging democratic empire. The United States certainly pressured its more traditional European allies to abandon explicit colonialist rela-tionships in developing nations, in favor of CIA-backed free-market influence, but few in the West ever pondered the issue of geographical balance on either side of the Iron Curtain.

This was the hidden dichotomy behind the BRUSA and UKUSA pacts. In later years, conservatives would express outright shock whenever the Soviets tried to establish listening posts in locations such as Cuba or Vietnam. Yet it was deemed perfectly acceptable to surround the Russian empire with antenna bases in nations such as Turkey, Pakistan, and Germany. Since radio interception and direction-finding were deemed to be passive activities, most developers within the secret agencies designing such systems felt that signals intelligence by its nature could not be considered provocative. Yet, because intelligence-platform siting policy was founded on the US concept of nuclear forward-basing, specific instances of building interception capability could only be seen as provocative by a paranoid Soviet leadership.

The notorious UKUSA Treaty, which has remained classified in the 56 years since its signing, assigned electronic snooping duties to five Caucasian, English-speaking nations. The United States was to monitor most of Europe, South America, the Atlantic, and the Soviet southern periphery. Britain was to take responsibility for Africa and the eastern Soviet Union. Canada was to establish over-the-horizon facilities to monitor polar regions of the north. Australia and New Zealand were to split monitoring missions in the Pacific. While the true signals-intelligence 'race for bases' by the US did not begin until well after the establishment of the National Security Agency in 1952, the US treated UKUSA as a starting pistol, and began signing secret base treaties with partners in Greece, Turkey, the Azores (Portugal), and the Philippines. In April 1949, the US agreed to pay for new signals bases established by other UKUSA members, such as Cheltenham in England and Gander in Canada.

The signals community in the United States had been reorganized twice in the aftermath of World War II in order to improve professionalism and efficiency. The Army Security Agency took charge of the Signal Security Agency at war's end, and the Armed Forces Security Agency was created in 1949 to provide equal weight to Navy and Air Force tasks. But the initial expertise of the AFSA during the first North Korean foray of the Korean War proved so dismal, a special commission under George Brownell was established to reorganize US interception and decryption talents. The NSA became the official successor to AFSA in November 1952.

In the wake of the first nuclear-armed bomber deployments from the US to Britain in 1948, plans were launched for establishing tiers of radar fences around the periphery of the Soviet Union, particularly in northern approaches to the United States from Canada. Again, because networks of radar were developed to monitor possible Soviet bomber intrusions, development of these networks was considered defensive at the time. Of course, the Soviets mimicked the US's activity in order to establish radar defensive lines against the American 'Silverplate' nuclear bombers. What few Americans knew until decades later was that American electronic intelligence planes specializing in games of 'chicken,' began regular probing missions as early as the winter of 1949–50, in which planes would deliberately enter Soviet air space in order to 'tickle' radar and receive information on Soviet radar signatures. Several recent works, such as James Bamford's *Body of Secrets*,[2] have documented the scores of pilots and technical specialists who were captured or killed during three decades of such missions. US Defense Department policy, initiated by Harry Truman's Secretary of Defense James Forrestal, was that under no circumstances would Soviet planes be allowed to make similar probes into US air defenses.

The point in examining such dangerous games is not to establish who was right or wrong, but to point out that signals intelligence can be probing and provocative, not merely a 'sit and listen' technology conducted in secret. Only in the past few years has the full extent of US expenditures and risk-taking in this realm been elucidated. In *Body of Secrets*, Bamford provided details on the multimillion-dollar signals stations established by both superpowers on ice floes in the Arctic Ocean. Because of the uncertain status of iceberg formation, such listening posts could not be expected to last more than a few years at best, yet they were regularly upgraded and replaced, particularly in the years when bombers were a bigger threat than missiles. Worse still, as the Air Force began expanding under President Eisenhower's administration, Ike opted for air tests far riskier than a single electronic intelligence plane flying into Soviet or Chinese airspace. Bamford describes a mission in early 1956 called Operation Homerun, in which scores of B-47s flew over the North Pole and penetrated several miles into Soviet airspace to simulate a nuclear attack. The purpose was to turn on enough Soviet radar and ELINT devices to create a military 'map' of the Soviet interior, yet there was little to distinguish Eisenhower's milk run from a legitimate nuclear attack.

Until internal Pentagon histories of computers and intelligence were released in the 1980s, few analysts understood how critical the NSA was to the early history of the commercial computer industry. And many analysts remain unaware, even today, how directly linked the NSA, air-defense radar developers, and computer developers were in the early 1950s. If one takes to heart the NSA mission of radio research, it should surprise few that a system for 'Radio Detecting And Ranging' should be at least a tangential NSA responsibility, yet the utility of radar in serving ground-based defenses for airborne intrusion led many to accept the cover story that radar networks were an air defense concern.

Prior to the dominance of missile-based nuclear warfare, defense against bombers represented the most important deterrent to nuclear war. The United States spent billions of dollars developing the Pine Tree radar line in the center of Canada, and the Distant Early Warning (DEW) radar system in northern Canada and Alaska. Tying it all together was SAGE, the Semi-Automatic Ground Environment. Without NSA basic research at locations such as MIT's Lincoln Labs, and without NSA financing of MIT programs like Whirlwind and Project Charles, there would have been no SAGE.

At first, NSA provision of funds to such companies as Raytheon, Technitrol, and Engineering Research Associates was used to develop special-purpose computers for applications in interception and decryption, delivered directly to NSA head-quarters in Fort Meade, Maryland. In the late 1940s, these 'Rapid Analytical Machines' were based on analog relays and vacuum tubes. These machines were single-purpose hard-wired platforms for code-breaking, not programmable computers. Later proposals put the NSA in the position of financing basic research in computer architectures. IBM received NSA money for the Harvest and Lightning projects, while Control Data Corp. virtually was created through venture funding from the NSA.[3]

The NSA simultaneously was financing basic research in antenna design and in long-range radar platforms. In the early 1950s, the agency came up with advances in the German Wullenweber antenna array (upright antennas shaped in concentric circles over a vast area, known colloquially as 'elephant cages'). The target-shaped antenna clusters could be used both in direction-finding, to pinpoint the location of a radio source, and in general interception of radio messages. There are four rings of antennas in a circular array 900 feet in diameter. The outermost ring intercepts high-frequency signals, while the second ring filters stray signals from the outer layer. The third ring of folded monopole antennas intercept low-frequency signals, while an inner fourth ring serves as a low-band reflector screen. The modernized version of Wullenweber, the Circularly Disposed Antenna Array, or FLR-9, was installed in several nations worldwide by NSA engineers during the late 1950s and 1960s.

The NSA work on long-range radar led to the construction of the AN/FPS-17 radar in Samsun, Turkey in 1955, with which the NSA could spy on Russian missile work in Kasputin Yar. Details on the Samsun radar were so sensitive, President Eisenhower denounced *Aviation Week & Space Technology* as 'treasonous' for revealing facts about it. The inability to analyze the take led to the NSA's first deep respect for telemetry as a separate technical discipline. A Telemetry and Beacon Analysis Committee (TeBAC) was formed to analyze signals received through Samsun, and members included future CIA satellite developer Albert 'Bud' Wheelon and future Secretary of Defense William Perry. More relevant to the intelligence and warfare topic, though, was the visit to Turkey by Joint Chiefs of Staff Deputy Director of Intelligence Edwin Layton in the spring of 1956. Layton denounced the artificial divisions created at the Turkey radar sites by Air Force, NSA, and other agencies, and suggested that treating communications intelligence, electronic intelligence, and radar management as separate tasks was 'counterproductive.'[4]

Given this general interest in radar technology, it should be no surprise that NSA was critical in driving the design of the Air Force's SAGE, and encouraged NATO to develop a similar system called NADGE (NATO Air Defense Ground Environment). SAGE used clusters of IBM AN/FSQ-7 computers, linked in to eight combat centers and 32 direction centers. Though ostensibly an Air Force system to defend against bomber attack, the first direction-center installation was at NSA headquarters. The theory behind SAGE, though it rarely worked well in practice, was to partition the United States into sectors, in which bomber activity would be monitored through civilian and military radar. Defenses against any real bomber penetration were rudimentary and often frightening – surface-to-air missiles with nuclear warheads were deployed in the suburbs of many American cities, often under the control of National Guard troops.

This surreal predecessor to missile defense was born in 1946, when the Air Defense Command was established at Mitchel Field, NY. Two years later, ADC was placed under the Continental Air Command (CONAD). In 1951, it was given a primary headquarters at Ent Air Force Base in Colorado Springs. As a short-range ground-based system intended for home defense, the ADC was managed by the Army, though the network was run with help from Air Force officials at Ent. The Pine Tree and DEW radar lines were placed under CONAD/ADC control, and both SAGE and the Ballistic Missile Early Warning System (BMEWS) later became part of this network.

Deployment of a two-stage conventional missile, Nike-Ajax, to most ADC bases, began in 1954. Like the SAGE control system, the Ajax battalion activations began with a Nike launcher at Fort Meade, home of the NSA. As part of the Pentagon fascination with all things nuclear, these batteries were upgraded with Nike-Hercules, a missile with a nuclear warhead, in 1958. Nike-Hercules had an effective range of 100 miles, and Pentagon planners believed it would suffice to defend against both bombers and intercontinental missiles, though many analysts doubted its ability to do much more than irradiate nearby surroundings. The nuclear missile batteries all had dedicated acquisition radar, called HiPAR, and companion tracking radar. The Army asked Bell Labs to develop a better ICBM-specific Nike, Nike-Zeus, in 1958, but problems in identifying Soviet ICBM characteristics prevented the Zeus from ever being deployed.

Because of the necessity of bringing Canada directly into the support of radar networks, the United States pressed to have the Continental Air Defense Command transformed into a binational command. But the resources were shared in name only. US officials could be nothing short of overbearing in their demands. During the spring of 1957, Canada temporarily halted intelligence-sharing, after US officials suggested that Canadian ambassador E. Herbert Norman had communist ties, and Norman subsequently committed suicide. The intelligence freeze ended with a change of government in Canada. After John Diefenbaker brought the conservatives into power in September 1957, Secretary of State John Foster Dulles demanded that NORAD (the North American Air Defense Command) be established without the approval of Canadian legislators. The primary

Western Hemisphere defense alliance thus was born in secrecy, in an atmosphere of bullying.

By 1959, the Air Force Security Service, a service element of NSA, had linked its radars at Samsun, as well as similar radars near Chaguaramas, Trinidad, and at the MIT Millstone Hill and CCM-1 projects, to the BMEWS and DEW radar networks. Lest this seem too arcane to cause furor, the mysterious murder of Merrill O'Donnell in Vancouver, BC, a DEW line engineer suspected of communist sympathies who was found dead of a gunshot wound in his hotel room in November 1958, serves as a reminder that radar siting and use constituted a very active and deadly part of the Cold War.

US use of British bases under the control of Britain's Government Communications Headquarters (GCHQ), the equivalent of the NSA, set the pattern for later dual-use bases worldwide, where a facility ostensibly under NASA, Navy, or Air Force control for scientific or defense purposes would be regularly utilized for intelligence purposes, by the NSA, GCHQ, or other UKUSA members. The British antenna fields in Singapore, Cyprus, Ascension Island, and other critical locations, became regular nodes in the NSA network. Long before space research was driven to the forefront by the Soviet Sputnik launch, the US Air Force and Navy were seeking facility rights throughout the Caribbean and British West Indies to set up radar tracking networks for sub-orbital missile flights. Many had dual intelligence functions.

As new technology was brought to bear on defense and monitoring networks, bases served similar double lives: the NSA and the new National Advisory Committee on Aeronautics (NACA, the future NASA) established Minitrack radar in Lima, Peru; Quito, Ecuador; Woomera, Australia; Zanzibar; and Esselen Park, South Africa. NACA and the Air Force shared time on Baker-Nunn cameras in Arequipa, Peru; Villa Dolores, Argentina; Naini-Tal, India; Cadiz, Spain; Curacao; Mitaka, Japan; and Olifanstfontein, South Africa.

The drive for this vast expansion of bases was the Soviet Union's success in developing first an atomic weapon, and later a rudimentary (though initially undeliverable) thermonuclear weapon. The early assumption that 'massive retaliation' could hold the Soviet Union at bay was dismissed as Soviet forces began deploying nuclear and signals forces first to the periphery of the Soviet Union itself, and then to its satellite states. There remained a significant difference in radius of concern, however: global dispersion of nuclear bombers and antenna fields by Western powers was always the right and proper thing to do, while extension of Soviet weapon systems to East Germany and Czechoslovakia brought panic to NATO planners, and immediate fears of the 'Fulda Gap' invasion nightmare. This is not to say that Soviet intentions were usually honorable; only that the gargantuan asymmetry evidenced in US power in the twenty-first century had its roots in a basic asymmetry of geographical spread that began in the early days of the Cold War.

The boasts of Soviet Premier Nikita Khrushchev led the worst-case analysts at the RAND Corporation to assume a 'bomber gap' that never existed, as US nuclear-capable bomber fleets remained well ahead of Soviet equivalents. But the desire to disprove the bomber gap was one of the factors that drove Eisenhower to approve the initial plan for a spy plane that could cross the Soviet land mass, and later for the vast expansion of the U-2 plane's bases. Given the degree to which Eisenhower was willing to lie to the Soviets and to his own people about his personal responsibility for planning U-2 flights, it is ironic that a primary reason for promoting the U-2 was to challenge conservatives' justifications for vastly expanding bomber fleets.

The obsession with watching Soviet bombers while developing air-breathing spy planes and long-range bombers does not mean US officials were blind to the potential of ballistic missiles. Indeed, the focal point of Project Paperclip, the effort to smuggle Nazi scientists to the US at the end of the war, was to establish a missile-development team at Redstone Arsenal in Alabama, a team that could leverage the early German work on the V-2 rocket. But conventional wisdom held that nuclear weapons could never be made light enough, nor rocket gyroscopic subsystems made accurate enough, to allow for a viable nuclear missile program before the end of the century.

It was only after a working H-bomb was demonstrated off Eniwetok Atoll in 1952 that the Teapot Committee, a strategic missiles evaluation group of the Atomic Energy Commission led by John von Neumann, recommended accelerated development of intercontinental ballistic missiles, or ICBMs, based on the Atlas rocket design. After initial radar data on Russian tests at Kasputin Yar was received from the NSA Samsun radar at the end of 1955, Atlas rocket development was accelerated to the highest national priority, and Martin Corp. was charged with developing a second rocket architecture, the Titan.

Launch of a world-circling satellite by the Soviet Union should have surprised no one, since public statements had been made by the Soviets throughout the spring and summer of 1957 regarding the successful tests of full-sized ICBMs. US Secretary of State John Foster Dulles had tacitly admitted the validity of the Soviet claims in late August, 1957, and the Pentagon followed up with an admission that four to six successful ICBM tests had been conducted. But to the American people, the milestone of a satellite, Sputnik-1, meant much more. The subsequent space race shifted efforts for space intelligence and communications dominance into high gear.

2
Civilian and Military Space Policies, Post-Sputnik

The United States' frantic but calamitous response to Sputnik would suggest from afar a nation that quickly molded a coherent civilian and military space effort from widely disparate constituent parts, yet failed to achieve the kind of results from that coherence that the Soviets were achieving. In reality, advances from predecessor agencies were more evolutionary than revolutionary, and the failure to achieve immediate successes was the result of years of treating space goals as targets for the very long term.

When the National Reconnaissance Office (NRO) went public in the mid-1990s with details of its 1960-era Corona program, the American public finally learned what was evident in the background for many years: The civilian space satellite program served as a cover for a wide-ranging spy satellite program. That came as little surprise to an academic community already accustomed to the idea that the civilian race to the moon had been little more than a Cold War stunt. In the aftermath of Sputnik, however, the creation of the National Aeronautics and Space Administration (NASA) from the remnants of the National Advisory Committee on Aeronautics assumed an aura of importance far greater than its worth.

Redstone Arsenal's politics had slowed the development of larger missiles during the 1950s, due to all-too-typical interservice struggles of the Air Force and Army. In 1956, the Air Force was given undisputed authority over ICBM development, while Army work was restricted to rocket systems of less than 200 miles' range. Partially as a result, Defense Secretary Neil McElroy chose the Army Nike program over the Air Force's Project Wizard in January 1958, as the first anti-missile program to move to partial deployment.

The Navy, meanwhile, was given authority for special space-tracking networks relevant to its mission, including the Space

Surveillance System, centered on an antenna field near Elephant Butte, New Mexico.

Following Sputnik, new agencies and technology efforts sprouted everywhere within the Department of Defense. The Advanced Research Projects Agency (ARPA, later DARPA) was created to centralize long-range R&D efforts throughout the Pentagon. More than $1 billion was allocated for missile and air-defense radar, and a special $189 million allocation was made to begin work on a Ballistic Missile Early Warning System, since program directors quickly realized that the DEW Line would be useless attempting to track ICBMs. Contracts were let in 1958 for BMEWS radars in Thule, Greenland and Shemya, Alaska. Fylingdales, England was selected as the primary European BMEWS site in November 1959, with four detection and three tracking radars planned for the Yorkshire Moors base.

Even the Naval Research Labs got into the radar budget race, receiving a grant from ARPA for Project TeePee, a 5–30 MHz radar for spotting ionized exhaust trails.

Space reconnaissance studies were promoted at low funding levels for several years prior to Sputnik, with the RAND Corp. fielding at least four theoretical papers between 1946 and 1955. The work was formalized in October 1956, when the Air Force assigned Lockheed to develop Weapon System 117L, known as the Pied Piper reconnaissance system. By 1958, Pied Piper had been funded to the tune of $12 billion, according to *Aviation Week* editor Philip Klass, and was slated to receive a much higher level of funding. The Army and CIA were invited to propose competitive systems, and the CIA's Project Corona was approved by the president in early 1958. Because of the CIA's early experience working with recoverable film capsules, the Corona design centered on use of a scanning camera with a film capsule that ejected from the satellite. Early work on Pied Piper had assumed the use of a radio-linked TV camera, though modem downlink times in that era were far too slow for radio transmission of either TV or scanned-camera images.[1]

Confusion arose in the early years of declassification as to the role of the Defense Department's 117L program, because it was split into Discoverer, Sentry/Pied Piper, and MIDAS (Missile Defense Alarm System) elements. Discoverer, promoted as a 'research and development' program, was a cover for the CIA's

Corona. Sentry, which later evolved into SAMOS, was preserved as a television-based alternative to Corona's scanning camera. And MIDAS was an infrared-based subsystem that was predecessor to both the Vela nuclear-detection satellite, and the Defense Support Program missile-launch detection system. Even in pre-launch days, the ties between reconnaissance and missile-defense systems were direct ones.

At first, expanding nuclear weapons platforms beyond the long-range bomber took precedence over replacing the U-2 for spying duties. The first nuclear submarine designed to carry nuclear missiles was launched in June 1959. In September of that year, the first Atlas missiles declared ready for nuclear-warfare duty were handed over to the Strategic Air Command at Vandenberg Air Force Base in California. Despite some unresolved problems with Atlas fuel valves, the US government could now claim to control a strategic nuclear 'triad' of bombers, submarines, and intercontinental missiles.

Not only was missile deployment deemed more imperative than spy satellite launches, but early Discover/Corona attempts were an embarrassment when compared to Soviet efforts. The first twelve Discoverer launches failed for a variety of reasons, and not until Discoverer 13 was a successful ocean retrieval of a film canister made. Unfortunately for the Eisenhower administration, during this time the era of direct overhead aerial reconnaissance came to an abrupt end when Francis Gary Powers' U-2 was shot down over Sverdlosk on May 1, 1960. As a direct result, Eisenhower ordered Defense Secretary Thomas Gates to reorganize military management of space reconnaissance, which led to the creation of the National Reconnaissance Office on August 25, 1960, and its evolution to independent form in September 1961. Joseph Charyk of the Air Force was named its first director. Though it became the largest intelligence agency by budget by the mid-1980s, the very existence of the agency was not declassified until 1992.

In some senses, the NRO served as a buffer between the CIA and Air Force, since the former agency had the responsibility for R&D, contracting, and security, while the Air Force provided the rockets, launching bases, ground stations, and recovery capabilities for spy satellites. Charyk set up three centers of excellence within the NRO, Program A serving the Air Force and internal NRO needs, Program B for the CIA, and Program C for the Navy.

Competition remained so intense between the Air Force and CIA, however, that a special Executive Committee on overhead reconnaissance, or EXCOM, was created to manage spying. The committee consisted of the Director of Central Intelligence, the Assistant Secretary of Defense, and the Presidential Science Advisor. On the satellite development front, the competition between the NRO and the CIA would erupt into virtual open warfare, where a dual track of satellite designing, meant to model the competition between Los Alamos and Lawrence Livermore nuclear design labs, instead became a bitter rivalry between the two intelligence agencies.

Luck in space began to change with the launch of Discoverer 14 on August 18, 1960, when photographs of an ICBM base at Plesetsk were recovered. Jeffrey Richelson, in a study of early space surveillance, claims that the salad days of Corona did not begin until mid-1961, when the series of launches between Discoverer 25 and Discoverer 31 gave the CIA's National Photographic Interpretation Center its first comprehensive set of photos of SS-6 ICBM missile sites in the Soviet Union.

The Air Force's Satellite and Missile Observation System, SAMOS, had a string of failures like Discoverer/Corona, but the program returned images with resolution ranging from 5 to 10 feet, beginning with SAMOS 5 in early 1962, ending with SAMOS 30, the last of the series, in late 1963. In the meantime, the NRO had changed the classified code names of both satellite systems after determining Corona and SAMOS had moved out of research phase. Imaging programs were given specific Keyhole, or KH numbers, with SAMOS designated KH-1 and Corona, KH-4.

In 1962, two classes of signals intelligence satellites were launched. One 'Ferret' class satellite, the first of what would become an entire family of 17 over nine years, was launched as the sole tenant of the second stage of a Thor-Agena B rocket, on May 15, 1962. The second class was the 'Piggyback Ferret' that shared launches with imaging satellites. Most such Ferrets moved from elliptical to circular orbits over a period of time, but Richelson claimed that some Ferrets were placed in particularly high circular orbits in the 1968–69 time frame, in order to specifically track Soviet Anti-Ballistic Missile radars. The tie between signals intelligence satellites and the ABM Treaty will be discussed later. Many of these satellites carried code names of famous celebrities, including Marilyn, Brigitte, and Raquel.

By the time the first of the Ferrets had launched, information on launches was getting hard to come by. Eisenhower had warned Kennedy that the U-2 repercussions suggested that the White House should err on the side of secrecy when discussing military satellites. SAMOS information was cut off from the public from the day Kennedy took office, and Air Force Gen. Bernard Schriever (for whom the satellite-control base in Colorado Springs was later named) was ordered to remove any mention of SAMOS from public speeches or testimony to Congress. After the Soviet Union began making more claims that satellite reconnaissance was inherently illegal, the NRO director declared in March 1962 that *all* Defense Department space activities should be considered classified.

Little information was released about the new Satellite Control Facility network, centered at the Blue Cube in Sunnyvale, California, at the southeast end of Moffett Field adjacent to Highways 101 and 237 (the control building later was renamed Onizuka Air Force Station, honoring Elison Onizuka, who perished in the 1986 *Challenger* disaster). Blue Cube was responsible for controlling virtually all military satellite systems from 1961 until the late 1990s, when most of its functions were taken over by Schriever Air Force Base in Colorado. Soon after the Sunnyvale station was completed in 1961, a series of remote tracking stations and monitoring facilities for spy satellites were set up at Vandenberg Air Force Base; New Boston, New Hampshire; Annette Island, Alaska; Kodiak Island, Alaska; Fort Greely, Alaska; Kaena Point, Hawaii; Fort Dix, New Jersey; and Camp Roberts, California. Additional sites were added at Thule, Greenland; Mahe, Seychelles; and Guam during the 1960s.

Richelson points out that the United States tried to have it both ways when President Kennedy issued National Security Action Memorandum 156 in May 1962. The memo called for the creation of an interagency committee on space under U. Alexis Johnson, to promote the value of overhead reconnaissance even while maintaining absolute secrecy. The committee recommendations called for talking up the peaceful nature of observation programs in international forums, and 'blurring the distinction between military and civilian space photography,' even while denying any information about military space programs. It is legitimate to conclude that by 1963, the basic tenets that were to lead to signing of the Outer Space Treaty of 1967 already had been violated: The treaty would allow for military networks in space that were not considered part of a weapon system. But if basic information about how the military network was used, who its beneficiaries were, and what were the technical capabilities of the equipment, were all classified, how could such assessments be made in any coherent fashion? Most nations chose not to ask the questions. As a result, networks already were in place at the time of the treaty's signing that made its conclusions all but useless.

The Soviet Union had little interest in directly challenging the legality of spy satellites, since it was meeting US capabilities by the second year of the Kennedy administration. Several satellites of the Cosmos series were launched in 1962, at least some of them returning images of the United States. This prepared the Soviets at least partially for the October missile crisis in Cuba, though Khrushchev had been chastened in similarly rash moves in Berlin when Kennedy informed him that US reconnaissance proved that the 'missile gap' was not nearly so much in the Soviets' favor as the Kremlin leadership wished Kennedy to believe.

The melding of U-2 and satellite-based reconnaissance data got its first exploitation during the Cuban missile crisis, when the EXCOM had to rely on a changing mix of *ad hoc* U-2 flights and 'national technical means of verification' to track the movement of Soviet missiles in the Cuban interior. (While the NRO supposedly remained classified until the 1990s, casual reference to the agency was made during the Cuba crisis and for several years after it, particularly in discussing Roswell Gilpatric's role in both the NRO and EXCOM. The agency was mis-identified, however, as merely a 'special office' within the Air Force.) Though the Powers shoot-down is often cited as the practical end of U-2 usefulness, it is important to remember that the U-2 and the later SR-71 reconnaissance plane had more than two decades of practical applications in Third World nations. In short, whenever a nation was not sophisticated enough to shoot down a reconnaissance plane, or powerful enough to challenge US power directly, the U-2 was used.

Kennedy may have been willing to take the United States closer to nuclear war than it had been before or has been since in the Cuban missile crisis, but his behavior was accepted by a majority of the American public as acceptable, because a majority of the population would not accept the existence of hostile nuclear missiles so close to the US border. Khrushchev's protestations that the Jupiter missiles in Turkey presented the same kind of threat played to deaf ears outside the Soviet satellite states, because asymmetry between the superpowers was considered acceptable. Even if the Kennedy actions in the missile crisis are seen as appropriate, however, the use of technical intelligence in this case was one of the last instances where US applications of imaging and signals intelligence could be judged as wholly defensive. The seeds of the 'tools of the warfighter' movement of the 1990s were sown in the constantly provocative actions Lyndon Baines Johnson took against national liberation struggles during his years as president.

The common team of Robert McNamara in Defense and the Bundy brothers in the National Security Council, preserved through both the Kennedy and the Johnson administrations, seemed tough but sober when dealing with an expanded threat of Soviet missiles, particularly when compared to the barbaric 'bomb first' views of 1964 Republican challenger Barry Goldwater. Yet the 'best and brightest' team signified all that was dangerous in the Cold War liberal point of view. Because of Kennedy's penchant for covert action, the growing use of radio research teams and tactical radar groups in South America and Southeast Asia was carried out in utmost secrecy. LBJ believed in brash displays of American power, so the electronic intelligence teams underpinning US expansion in Vietnam, Laos, Cambodia, the Dominican Republic, Brazil and elsewhere were introduced in an open, brazen fashion.

Common to both administrations was the view of Robert McNamara, who believed, even prior to the Cuban missile crisis, in the kind of expansionist Soviet Union that the ultra-rightists around Ronald Reagan would warn of 20 years later under the auspices of the Committee on the Present Danger. McNamara, in the early years of the Kennedy administration, encouraged studies of the potential for taking out Soviet nuclear forces in a debilitating first strike, but determined that it would be impossible to do so even assuming a vast expansion of US nuclear capabilities. He subsequently advocated force modernization for all three legs of the nuclear triad, but doubted the wisdom of expanding the Sentinel/Safeguard program of missile defense. These doubts would surface in 1967 as US and Soviet negotiators opened ABM discussions.

In later years, McNamara expressed regret for assisting in the nuclear buildup that was a natural consequence of a global struggle by proxy. Yet he never seemed to realize that the Defense Department's role in seeing all developing-nation struggles through an East–West lens, and his own insistence on aggressively pursuing possible insurgent activity in any corner of the world, was at least as dangerous and provocative as the expansion of nuclear arsenals.

Several studies of the Vietnam War, and of US counterinsurgency operations in Latin America, have covered in great detail the vast and expensive use of signals intelligence in tactical operations. When specific listening posts like Monkey Mountain in Vietnam were protected 'at all costs,' the waste of resources approached the levels of the CIA's abuse of covert funding in arming secret armies in Laos. More important to the thesis herein, however, is the regular and sustained abuse of signals intelligence for achieving US goals that were determined in advance. In the well-known case of manufacturing evidence of a North Vietnam patrol boat attack in the Tonkin Gulf in August 1964, for example, fraud existed on many levels. North Vietnam forces never fired torpedoes at the *Maddox* and *Turner Joy*, two electronic intelligence ships engaged in interception activities of questionable legality. In any event, the two ships were monitoring the guerilla activities of shore-based South Vietnam teams in North Vietnam, run by the CIA and Defense Department operation called OPLAN34A. And many analysts claim that the guerillas involved in OPLAN34A, charged with dynamiting North Vietnam radar and intelligence posts, were deliberately dropped off in the wrong location by US agents, so that their movements could be tracked by North Vietnamese electronic sources, providing a trove of information to the *Maddox* and *Turner Joy*. All too often, in Vietnam and elsewhere, the Pentagon was not engaged in a single layer of deception, but multiple layers of provocative and treacherous behavior meant to aid intelligence collection.

Throughout the Johnson administration, McNamara tried to balance military and civilian interests within the NSA. He also worked at bringing missile-warning and signals intelligence functions closer together. While this provided a network that would prove more useful than the visible warning network of the DEW Line, BMEWS, and the NORAD underground command center inside Cheyenne Mountain, it set the stage for the conversion of the intelligence community from treaty verification to warfighting, which accelerated rather overtly in the 1990s.

NSA Director Marshall 'Pat' Carter, who served during the height of the Vietnam buildup from 1965 to 1969, wanted to keep the direction of the NSA clearly in civilian hands, to prevent the agency from being over-burdened with tactical analysis duties (which did indeed take place following the Cold War). His advocacy helped to keep strategic intelligence focused first on Soviet and Chinese analysis that aided the White House and civilian leadership, and only secondarily on the tactical struggles of the developing world. But the Pentagon continually complained of being all but prevented from defining Vietnam missions for the NSA, and when Navy Adm. Noel Gayler took over the NSA in 1969, the pendulum swung back to the military, at least through Nixon's first term and the turn toward 'Vietnamization' of the war.

Even as consideration for limiting anti-missile technology was taking place within McNamara's Defense Department, initial successes in the MIDAS and Vela warning satellites during 1965–66 led to early planning for the Code 647 Defense Support Program (DSP) satellite, a system that would combine elements of missile early-warning, nuclear explosion detection, and multi-frequency signals intelligence. Even when programs were considered worthwhile, though, development and procurement budgets were delayed by the black hole of the Vietnam War effort. Four years elapsed between a very successful follow-on to MIDAS, then called Project 461, and the first launch of a true Defense Support Program 647 satellite in November 1970.

By the mid-1960s, an international site-selection committee was scoping out three continents for ground stations to serve as DSP downlinks. A new site near Woomera, Australia, an existing

Army Security Agency listening post at Menwith Hill, England near Harrogate, and a tactical air command base in Aurora, Colorado called Buckley Air National Guard Field were chosen by 1966 as the future homes of the downlinks. At all three locations, additional radomes for signals intelligence downlinks, as well as antennas for Earth-based interception, joined the DSP support radomes within a matter of months. Ideally, the Pentagon always demanded multi-function bases in order to save money. A site near Alice Springs for a signals-intelligence and image-intelligence-relay ground station, called Merino or Pine Gap, had been chosen in 1969, so the separate DSP station at Nurrungar was added virtually as an afterthought, with the assumption that two Australian bases being sought at the same time would create less furor than two requests spaced a few years apart. Buckley won out over sites in Iowa or Colorado Springs, in part because the NRO had chosen Buckley as a downlink for its Jumpseat signals intelligence satellites. Menwith Hill, meanwhile, was becoming the catch-all base for a variety of NSA and NRO functions in Great Britain.

Because DSP was designed specifically for alerting national forces to possible ICBM launches from the Soviet Union, its potential to take on other duties was not realized until other missions were mandated following the fall of the Soviet Union in 1991. In retrospect, important intelligence information from early DSP tests was tossed away or ignored. Carl Fischer, vice president and general manager of space sensors at Northrop-Grumman Corp., said in a 2003 speech that 'the past experience from DSP is that the best story was on the cutting-room floor.' Each satellite was considered only for its independent operation, Fischer said, so the advantages of stereoscopic observation were bypassed. Similarly, DSP's ability to see static events like forest fires was not recognized until the 1990s.[2]

The evolution to the second generation of imaging and signals intelligence satellites might have taken a quantum leap during the Vietnam War years, due to whiz kid Bud Wheelon's assignment to the new Office of Science and Technology at the CIA, were it not for his problems dealing with other agencies, which hindered his overall impact. Wheelon spurred some core concepts in the use of geosynchronous satellite placement and charge-coupled devices for imaging,[3] though opinions are mixed as to how he followed through ideas to implementation. Studies by Richelson and Philip Taubman credit Wheelon with coming up with the basic concepts for the KH-9 Hexagon or Big Bird imaging satellite, the later KH-11 Crystal, which was the first true digital-readout imaging satellite, and the geosynchronous Rhyolite signals intelligence satellite. Yet all three were delayed in part by bitter rivalries between the CIA and the NRO, particularly in the mid-1960s, when Brockway McMillan headed the NRO. After Wheelon's departure in 1966, the CIA and NRO rivalry regained a sense of healthy competition, which spawned the design race between the CIA-backed Magnum/Orion/Mentor programs, and the NRO-backed Chalet/Vortex/Mercury.

But between 1962 and 1965, inter-agency relations were at breaking point. McMillan refused to sign a Memorandum of Understanding to ease CIA/NRO disputes in May 1962, and in March 1965, he canceled a Corona launch in a dispute with the CIA. McMillan was dismissed as NRO head in the summer of 1965 as a result of this flap, and incoming CIA Director William Raborn strongly supported a continuing role for the CIA in satellite design.[4]

While this rivalry was influencing the expansion of US space-support bases in the Australian outback, the NSA and Defense Intelligence Agency needed a dedicated network that could provide more integrated early warning than was possible with the NORAD system. In September 1966, the Defense Special Missile and Aeronautics Center was opened at NSA headquarters. To this day, DEFSMAC remains one of the most highly-classified operations in the intelligence community. Presaging the intelligence 'fusion' that would be offered to tactical battle groups in the 1990s, DEFSMAC fused together intelligence from several sources to provide a comprehensive view of the planet and any advance activity from another nation that would seem to anticipate a missile attack. It is no accident that the commanders of NORAD began to give public tours of Cheyenne Mountain in the 1970s, and allow filming of its command center for entertainment purposes. By 1970, NORAD represented only the public face of missile warning, and remained a rather outdated public face through the end of the century. The real eyes and ears for missile-defense systems were opened during the Nixon administration at Pine Gap, Nurrungar, Menwith Hill, and Buckley, serving the DEFSMAC nerve center at NSA known only to a few.

3
Star Wars Part 1:
Safeguard, ABM, and Intelligence
Struggles in Space

Few limitations on nuclear weapons development were recognized or respected in the period bounded by the launch of Sputnik and the opening of Anti-Ballistic Missile Treaty discussions in 1967. It is no coincidence that this period corresponds with the years of Nikita Khrushchev's reign as Soviet premier, since his rash rhetoric and rasher actions often provoked worst-case analysis among US strategic analysts. But it is equally true that Eisenhower, Kennedy, and Johnson all rejected many excuses for limiting land-based ICBMs, even after realizing that long-feared bomber gaps and missile gaps did not exist. Whenever a new form of nuclear weapon or delivery vehicle could be developed, it *was* developed.

As quickly as thermonuclear weapons were transformed from 'boosted fission' devices to a deliverable two-stage fusion weapon, they were adopted as key elements of land and sea missiles, as well as long-range bombers. H-bombs were given smaller yields for tactical use, but also were boosted in yield to create monstrous city-busters with explosive capacity measured in tens of megatons. Neither the United States nor the Soviet Union showed the slightest hesitancy to test such weapons in the atmosphere, one factor leading to the growth of the ban-the-bomb movement in North America and Europe in the late 1950s.

Protesters made few differences to strategic planning among Western nations, however. In fact, one element that finally pushed Kennedy administration officials to a partial test ban was the decline in image quality in certain Corona satellite film returns after spy satellites flew through a radiation belt created in the Starfish series of nuclear tests. Designers working on missile-warning satellites of the MIDAS/DSP class also worried about possible 'red-out' of infrared data if satellites were attacked with

nuclear weapons, or went through radiation belts. Possible environmental effects of exoatmospheric testing could be ignored, but
once intelligence was affected, the superpowers got serious about
limiting nuclear testing.

Expenditures on offensive weapons, as well as on the conventional force expansion needed for Vietnam and other
counterinsurgency operations, kept the Pentagon from moving
the Nike-Hercules program into legitimate production, though
its capabilities were not given high priority under McNamara,
because Nike was not seen as a legitimate foil against intercontinental ballistic missiles. The problem was not just missiles used
in the Nike ABM network. Studies of electromagnetic pulse
problems conducted in the early 1960s convinced the Pentagon
that the radars used in both Nike-Hercules and Nike-Zeus would
be blinded, even by moderate EMP levels, during a nuclear
exchange.

Interest in missile defense remained high, however, because
information from the NSA Samsun radar in Turkey indicated that
the Soviet Union had conducted its first successful interception
test against an ICBM in March 1961. In 1963, ARPA conducted a
'Project Defender' study, which advocated using a modified
version of the Nike-Zeus-B rocket, dubbed the Nike-EX for 'exoatmospheric,' along with a shorter-range missile called Sprint. By
October 1965, the first contract for the Nike-EX program was let,
which called for development of missile-defense sites, surrounding both cities and ICBM fields. These sites typically were
comprised of the Nike-EX and Sprint missiles, along with two
radar systems: the Perimeter Acquisition Radar with a 1,000-mile
range, and a 'last-ditch' radar to be used in conjunction with the
Sprint missile, the Raytheon Missile-Site Radar with integrated
array. These systems represented the first application of the new
phased-array radars, in which active beams could be formed by
artificially 'steering' a signal across an array of solid-state radio-
frequency modules. These elements would use complex
mathematical algorithms to decide on relative strengths of the
radar signal, so that a flat-faced radar could steer a beam as effectively as a revolving-dish radar. The phased-array radar later
formed the basis for several major programs, including the
BMEWS upgrades at Fylingdales and other sites, and the PAVE
PAWS radars on the east and west coasts of the United States.

(PAVE is an Air Force program name; PAWS stands for Phased Array Warning System.)

McNamara finally was pushed into making a decision on ABM production in mid-1967, after the Soviet Union had deployed the first field of Galosh anti-missile missiles around Moscow. Because diplomats still were trying to convince Premiere Kosygin of the value in limiting ABM weapons, the public justification for moving forward with Nike-EX (renamed Sentinel by McNamara) was the concern about China's nuclear capability and its testing of intermediate-range missiles. The real concern remained the USSR, of course, though it was impolitic to say so, and easier to use China as the rogue state, since Mao Zedong was in the midst of the throes of the Cultural Revolution. The initial network of Sentinel sites carried a price tag of $5 billion in 1967 dollars, though critics in Congress anticipated the figure to increase by at least 40 per cent.

While citizen opposition to ABM weapons usually took a back seat to Vietnam and civil rights issues, serious and fundamental questioning of ABM strategy was part of mainstream consciousness at least as early as 1962, when *Scientific American* published a major critique of the technology. After McNamara announced the initial sites for the Sentinel system, major protests erupted in 1968 in such locations as Seattle, Boston, and Chicago. As a result, incoming Republican President Richard Nixon suspended work on Sentinel in February 1969, though he proposed a 12-site version of essentially the same system in March 1969, renamed Safeguard.

By this time, opposition to ABM was significant enough that Vice President Spiro Agnew had to serve as tie-breaker on an initial ABM vote in Congress in late 1969. In Nixon's Safeguard architecture, two ABM fields were to be built to guard ICBM fields at Malmstrom Air Force Base in Montana, and Grand Forks Air Force Base in North Dakota. This was to be followed by a second phase at Whiteman Air Force Base in Missouri and Warren Air Force Base in Wyoming. Because the Grand Forks construction was far ahead of Malmstrom, when the ABM Treaty and accompanying Strategic Arms Limitation Talks I accords were signed in 1972, all work on the Malmstrom site was halted.

Moving anti-missile systems into production required additional radar development work at the splashdown site in the

Pacific Ocean used for missile testing, already a bustling Air Force and Army facility for ICBM tests. Kwajalein Atoll had an unfortunate history in the 1960s and 1970s that resembled the abusive and neo-colonialist history experienced by the natives of other Marshall Islands and nearby US trust territories when nuclear testing took place in the Pacific in the 1940s and 1950s. In the case of Kwajalein, residents were not willing to go as quietly as the residents of Bikini, Eniwetok, and other islands did in the early years of the Cold War. Roi Namur island in the Kwajalein Atoll was cleared out to make room for a series of new radars, but residents attempted reoccupation actions through the end of the century.

Among the new facilities at Kwajalein serving ABM interests were three major test radars, part of ARPA's Pacific Range Electromagnetic Signature Study (PRESS) program. The ARPA Long-Range Tracking and Instrumentation Radar, or ALTAIR, was a 150-foot observation radar capable of serving a variety of ABM and space intelligence interests. The ARPA-Lincoln (Labs) Coherent Observable Radar, ALCOR, was a specialized C-band radar optimized for observing small re-entry vehicles. The Hard Point Demonstration Array Radar, or HAPDAR, was a special phased-array test platform meant to demonstrate expansion of phased arrays to intercontinental missile warning. By the twenty-first century, Kwajalein operations had been normalized to the point that the collection of analysis and processing facilities on the atoll had gained the official name 'Ronald Reagan Missile Defense Test Site.' At the time, however, Kwajalein expansion was taking place far from public awareness, similar to the way test radar boomed on the Hawaiian islands of Kauai and Ni'ihau in the 1990s without public knowledge.

By the waning days of the Johnson administration, an increasing number of high-frequency military communication tasks were moving to space. The Pentagon had attempted to shift many of its *ad hoc* terrestrial communication networks to a dedicated, packet-switched DoD-specific precursor to the Internet called 'WWMCCS' (Worldwide Military Command and Control System), but the network was hindered by both the experimental state of packet-switched data networking at the time, and the natural Balkanization of service-specific military networks. To help aid the veritable explosion in tactical communications experienced during the Vietnam War, the military began launching 26-MHz Defense Satellite Communication System (DSCS) program satellites in the summer of 1967. The first 26 satellites were launched in four groups by Titan III-C launchers, into near-equatorial orbits 18,300 miles high. At the time, designers planned to only test the ability to receive data, video and voice, using low-speed frequency-shift-keyed modems. These were followed by the more robust DSCS-2 satellites, 14 of which were launched between 1971 and 1982; and the longer-life DSCS-3, which offers better jam resistance and operates at Super-High Frequency, between 7.25 and 8.4 GHz. There have been more than ten DSCS-3 launches between 1982 and 2003, with at least nine active satellites in a higher, geosynchronous orbit than the initial DSCS satellites.

One of the highest-priority satellite programs in the Nixon Defense Department was Project 647, the follow-on to MIDAS known as Defense Support Program or DSP. Intended to watch for missile launches and possible nuclear explosions through a series of infrared sensors, DSP was designed as a multifunction platform with a decidedly defensive purpose – at least, until it was re-purposed for tactical battle in the early 1990s. Prior to the first DSP launch in late 1970, the US established control and downlink bases for the satellites at Nurrungar, Australia, and Buckley Air National Guard Field in Aurora, Colorado. The new radome sites also involved personnel from the NSA and the NRO, since the two bases also were used as downlinks for the elliptical-orbit 'close-listen' Jumpseat electronic intelligence satellites. This was all the more appropriate because Jumpseat, and its later successor Trumpet, carried a secret infrared package called Heritage that extended and enhanced the capabilities of the DSP system.

Both the signals intelligence and photographic intelligence satellite programs moved to a more stable base of large platforms in the late 1960s. Signals intelligence development took an odd, tri-partite path that stemmed as much from NRO and CIA rivalries discussed earlier, as from genuine debates about capabilities. One category of elliptical-orbit, hovering satellite that evolved into the Jumpseat or Trumpet series, was agreed upon by all designers as a necessary gapfiller system to intercept communications in high latitudes, and in special frequency bands.

But for microwave, Very High Frequency, and Ultra High Frequency communications picked up by satellites in geosynchronous or geostationary orbits, the NRO (with support from the NSA) and the CIA did not see eye to eye. The NSA believed in dedicated microwave interception satellites, which had their first instantiation in the Canyon or Spook Bird satellites launched between 1968 and 1970. TRW Corp., the prime contractor for several later production geosynchronous satellites, built the first three developmental Canyon satellites, which occupied inclined orbits of 19,000 by 25,000 miles high, and had antennas 3 meters wide. These satellites gave rise to the family known variously over time as Chalet, Vortex, or Mercury (spy satellites would change code names as soon as an earlier code name was compromised). The first Canyon satellites launched required a European ground station, established at Bad Aibling, Germany in 1968. When this program was expanded to the larger Chalet program in 1970, the existing NSA base at Menwith Hill near Harrogate was expanded for downlinking duties under Project P-285.

The CIA's Office of Signals Intelligence insisted that a single satellite could perform multi-frequency analysis. The agency contracted with TRW Corp. for development of the Rhyolite satellite, and initiated land development of a ground station at Pine Gap, Australia, near Alice Springs.

Similarly, photographic intelligence had to await the improvement of charge-coupled devices to allow for all-digital imagery used in the KH-11 Kennan/Crystal class of spy satellite. However, the high-resolution, close-look KH-8 Gambit and lower-resolution area-surveillance KH-9 Hexagon satellites launched in the early 1970s represented a substantial improvement over Corona. By making detailed global mapping (at resolutions far greater than NASA's Landsat) a regular part of the intelligence game, these initial missions placed future agencies like Defense Mapping Agency and the National Imagery and Mapping Agency, fully within the mission reach of space-based warfare. While KH-9 made use of multi-spectral scanners, it still had to rely on film ejection. Given that KH-9 satellites played a role in strategic intelligence until the mid-1980s, it is surprising to some students of the Corona mission that digital image transmission did not fully replace film ejection until Reagan's second term in office.

The missing KH-10 was the designation given to the earliest proposals for continuous manned reconnaissance, the Manned Orbiting Laboratory. Even though a few ideas from the MOL survived in the short-lived Skylab mission of the mid-1970s, cost escalations for meeting the initial MOL project goals (which were never about general science, and always solely about reconnaissance) had gotten so severe by 1969, Nixon and Laird canceled the program. The CIA's warning that the Soviet Union would object to manned overhead reconnaissance also played a part in killing the program.

While no one in the Nixon or Ford administrations displayed the same fascination for technical intelligence that Jimmy Carter showed when he appointed Stansfield Turner to the CIA and Bobby Ray Inman to the NSA in 1977, the Republican years were critical ones for expanding space-based intelligence programs, as well as for developing the theories that put space communications and intelligence at the service of direct battlefield tasks. It is an open question how consciously the executive branch expanded space military systems to create the same shift from countervalue to counterforce strategy inherent in nuclear weapons development, but the sharper arms analysts outside the government had figured out what was going on by the end of the 1970s.

Nixon's National Security Advisor Henry Kissinger, rightfully seen as a Machiavellian power-broker in many venues, at least had a more sober view of Soviet intent than the strongest proponents of ABM deployment in the United States. Kissinger recognized the value of the Multiple Independently-Targeted Re-entry Vehicle, or MIRV, as a means of multiplying the number of targets that could be hit by any individual missile. Because US developers were far ahead of their Russian counterparts at developing true MIRVs, the issue of numbers of missiles or their size and relative 'throw weight' were of less interest to Kissinger and Defense Secretary Melvin Laird than they were to extreme defense hawks in the military and Congress (many of whom were, like Senator Henry Jackson, Democrats rather than Republicans). Consequently, the main concerns driving the US negotiators during SALT I talks were not restraining Soviet heavy missiles, but keeping both sides from starting a new arms race with defensive missiles. In addition to having the ABM Treaty as its centerpiece, the SALT I treaty included a preliminary strategic arms-reduction agreement which locked in a certain Soviet advantage in heavy missiles.

While there had been talk of trying to pre-emptively ban MIRVs as part of SALT I, negotiator Gerard Smith claimed in his memoirs that the Soviets would have been forced into accepting inspections of anti-aircraft sites, and of possibly dismantling Soviet phased-array radars as part of such a ban, and thus they showed no interest in a MIRV ban. In any event, Kissinger and the Joint Chiefs were united in believing that MIRV deployment and electronics miniaturization in US missiles would more than make up for any Soviet advantage in missile size.

In other elements of the SALT talks, Kissinger and the Joint Chiefs did not see eye to eye. The Pentagon remained insistent that Soviet work on phased-array radar be curtailed, despite the fact that the US had several phased-array radars in its early-warning network. Gerard Smith and Secretary of State William Rogers were especially adamant that Soviet radars be limited by location, antenna-type, and a measure of effective power called the power-aperture product. They were both outraged that Kissinger constantly was going behind their backs, working out less onerous radar deals in private with Soviet leaders.[1]

Kissinger's regular habit of undercutting Rogers and concluding deals through back channels had a blowback effect on defense hardliners, particularly in the archaic Goldwater wing of the Republican Party, and among the Democrat neo-conservatives exemplified by Jeane Kirkpatrick and Irving Kristol. As early as the first term of the Nixon administration, the hardline crew who would later form the Committee on the Present Danger claimed that Nixon was selling out missile defense in the name of détente. Some of the first suggestions that greater Soviet missile throw-weight represented 'breakout' into first-strike policies, were made by analysts around Paul Nitze and Richard Perle at this time.

But who was showing the greater interest in striking first? The US political wing in favor of broad Safeguard deployment tended to be the same people who were arguing for preventing the Soviets from conducting any research in phased-array radar. These particular hawks claimed that the Soviets were planning on a massive first strike against the US and its allies. Occasionally, the far right could point to legitimate Soviet duplicity in complying with the ABM Treaty, as in the 1980s case of the Krasnoyarsk multi-faceted early-warning radar. But all too often the anti-SALT clique did not let truth stand in its way. Ret. Gen. George Keegan, for example, beat the drum throughout the 1970s over an alleged Soviet particle-beam weapon being tested at Saryshagan, a weapon which, all evidence suggests, never existed.

These claims were being made precisely at a time when US Poseidon subs were beginning regular patrols in the Indian Ocean for the first time; when US Los Angeles-class subs under the control of the Navy liaison office to the NSA were being tasked with snooping on Soviet undersea cable in the 'Ivy Bells' missions; and when the US and Britain were making strides in upgrading new forward-projection bases in Diego Garcia and Ascension. NSA listening posts on the borders of eastern Europe were being massively upgraded with fully automated systems, under the expensive classified programs called La Faire Vite, LeFox Grey, LeFox Green, and LeFox Purple. And new US strategic weapons being discussed throughout Washington included the MX MIRVed missile and its shell-game deployment scheme, the D-5 sea-launched missile and its new Trident submarine, the B-1 bomber, and the Pershing and cruise missile intermediate-range launchers for the European theater.

Robert Aldridge, a Trident missile engineer at Lockheed, was one of the first analysts to suggest that this confluence of capabilities would look to an outsider like a deliberate effort by the US to strike first. In a pamphlet from the Institute for Policy Studies that made a big splash in the nascent anti-nuclear community of the 1970s, *The Counterforce Syndrome*, Aldridge argued that US planners had abandoned mutually assured destruction theory when the Single Integrated Operational Plan (SIOP) for nuclear war began to emphasize counterforce, or the targeting of hardened silos, over countervalue, or the targeting of cities. Perhaps this was not deliberate, but a case of technological 'creep' allowing a more accurate nuclear weapon to hit targets that could not have been considered in the early 1960s. The effect on doctrine was the same, Aldridge said, regardless of conscious intent or announced intent: the United States was moving to a first-strike policy of nuclear weapons use.[2]

The respected Australian arms researcher Desmond Ball, watching the disputes in his nation's parliament during the early 1970s over the siting of a signals intelligence satellite downlink station at Pine Gap and a DSP early-warning station at Nurrungar, extended the tacit first-strike concept to intelligence platforms. Ball warned that the shift of intelligence platforms to outer space, their ability to transmit information in real-time, and the ability of ground stations to fuse intelligence from signals, imaging, and other sources, created a situation in which intelligence systems of the future would support provocative first-strike actions, not the verification activities that formed the basis of arms control. Unless someone paid attention to 'technological creep' in the intelligence community, Ball said, the results by the turn of the century could be very unpleasant. His 1980 book on Pine Gap and Nurrungar which elucidated this point, *A Suitable Piece of Real Estate*, was ignored at the time, and its specific warnings discounted until the arrival of nakedly pre-emptive warriors in Washington early in the twenty-first century.[3]

While Nixon and his successor, Gerald Ford, had several opportunities to proceed with caution in both MIRV development and intelligence-base evolution in the mid-1970s, the intransigence of Kissinger in coping with rebellion in the developing world prevented such options from being exercised. To Kissinger, any disruption in strategic networks served as prima-facie evidence of Soviet meddling in the Third World. There was little Kissinger and Nixon could do in 1973–74 to stanch the fatal rot overwhelming the South Vietnamese government. But as the old colonialist network of European nations crumbled in the 1970s, Kissinger did not miss a chance to prop up allied intelligence infrastructure – in Greece and Cyprus, in former Portuguese colonies from the Azores to Angola, in East Timor and Indonesia, and in Iraq and Iran. Even advanced industrial-nation allies were not immune from dirty tricks, as Australian Prime Minister Gough Whitlam was to discover at the end of 1975 (see pp. 42–3). Assumptions that the Soviet Union spurred all revolutionary rhetoric in the developing world led to a vicious and negative circle: expansion of US foreign bases led to more turmoil, which caused Kissinger and the presidents he served to assume more hidden roles for Moscow, which led to a tougher line in nuclear weapon development and deployment. And of course, Nixon and Ford both were pressured by the Republican right, whose members assumed that all détente and openings to China were proof of the US selling out to Communists.

The hidden shenanigans by the Kissinger team in small nations that played host to signals intelligence bases had lasting impact through the end of the century. It set the stage for Jimmy Carter's later perceived losses in Iran and elsewhere, which helped propel Ronald Reagan to power. It forced tighter collaboration between the NRO and the NSA, with the latter agency hoping for better geosynchronous listening satellites that could replace ground bases in sensitive locations. And overt acts like the removal of Australian PM Gough Whitlam set the stage for the extremely aggressive posture of the intelligence community in the 1980s and 1990s, broken only by a brief and partial interlude during the Carter years.

The toughest problems for the signals intelligence community in the mid-1970s centered on North Africa, the Horn of Africa, and the Eastern Mediterranean, the result of the collapse of the Portuguese colonial empire, and of the Greek–Turkish impasse following Turkey's invasion of Cyprus. Kissinger played an active role in assembling private interests to launch an unsuccessful Front for the Liberation of the Azores, in order to separate the critical Azores Islands bases from the Portuguese military junta, leaning increasingly to the left throughout 1974. Lajes in the Azores played host to an Air Force Security Service base, a Naval Security Group antenna field, and a sound surveillance system (Sosus) support base for the undersea arrays that listened for Soviet submarines. The Portuguese junta's desire to rid itself of colonies later would threaten more peripheral UKUSA signals bases in Cape Verde, East Timor, Papua New Guinea, and Angola.

Lajes in the Azores assumed a greater importance in the anti-Portugal campaign, because the US was in the process of losing its critical Kagnew listening post in Ethiopia, following Emperor Haile Selassie's removal by the Marxist Dergue. The Eritrean People's Liberation Front actually presented a greater threat to Kagnew's operation than the Dergue, since EPLF controlled the territory surrounding Kagnew, and the Dergue entertained thoughts of retaining the US base at least temporarily. But the NSA, perhaps wisely, doubted the Dergue's long-term intent, and began winding down the Kagnew post by the time of Nixon's resignation. Unfortunately for the NSA, the Ethiopia phase-out happened concurrently with the Soviet expansion of a naval signals base at Berbera in the neighboring nation of Somalia. In reality, Berbera never approached the importance of US naval signals bases like Diego Garcia during its three years under the Soviets, but it allowed conservatives to make great hay regarding 'losing the Horn of Africa to the Soviets.'

In Cyprus, Kissinger's insistence on promoting pro-Greek rightists like Nikos Sampson led perversely to a three-way political loss: the demise of the Cyprus-based EOKA-B Greek nationalist movement; the removal of the neutralist leader of Cyprus, Archbishop Makarios; and the resignation of the ruling junta on the Greek mainland. When Turkey invaded Cyprus in July 1974 to stem a secessionist movement to return the island to Greece, members of the US Congress were incensed at Kissinger's role in promoting provocative actions that led to the invasion. US and British listening posts at Akrotiri and Ayios Nikolaos on Cyprus, critical in monitoring the 1973 Yom Kippur War, were threatened with permanent closure. The Greek government severely restricted two listening posts on the island of Crete: the Air Force Security Service base at Iraklion, and the Naval Security Group base at Nea Makri. But the biggest losses were in Turkey. When Congress froze military funds to Turkey to protest the invasion, the Turkish government responded by closing seven critical US intelligence bases, and putting severe restrictions on how any remaining operations could be utilized by the NSA. Even after the arms embargo was lifted in early 1980 and the bases reopened, Turkey demanded much tougher terms on sharing information from US listening posts.

In the brief period in Nixon's second term before the president had to spend all waking hours fighting for his political life, he was promulgating the Nixon Doctrine, handing over to regional authoritarian rulers the primary responsibility of protecting US interests. This doctrine dissolved under the North Vietnam and Pathet Lao onslaughts in Southeast Asia, but it came to practical use in replacing the Turkey losses, in the waning days of the Nixon administration. The Shah of Iran helped insure that much information collected from Turkish bases on Soviet military activity could be replaced, not only through the expansion of Iranian NSA bases in Kabkan and Klarabad, but through the

Shah's contracting of private ('sheep-dipped') NSA and CIA agents in the development of allegedly domestic intelligence projects such as Ibex, Peace Crown, and Peace Owl. Dependence upon the Shah to make up for closed Turkish bases made it harder, of course, for the Carter administration to pull away from the Shah in 1979.

Right-wingers within the new Ford administration, including Daniel Graham and Erich Von Marbod, wanted to go further in supporting overtly rightist global coalitions than Kissinger and incoming CIA Director George H.W. Bush were willing to go. The CIA and the NSA were quite reticent to chum up to the Pinochet regime's efforts to finance a multi-state death squad out of Chile, Operation Condor. And the US tried to deflect conservatives' demands that more American money go into the expansion of the Silvermine signals intelligence base in South Africa, a project called Advocaat. Private supporters of Advocaat tried to promote the concept of the base being ideal for both intelligence and missile-defense testing.

One instance where the NSA showed the degree to which it would stoop to match CIA agents' dirty tricks was in the removal of Australian Prime Minister Gough Whitlam, taken out in a 'constitutional coup' on November 11, 1975, engineered on CIA and NSA orders. It bears emphasis that Whitlam was not the hero of progressive interests some would make him out to be. He played a very furtive pro-Indonesian role in helping to grease the skids for an Indonesian invasion of East Timor in late 1975, primarily by providing intelligence to Indonesia from the Defence Signals Directorate's listening post at Shoal Bay. Whitlam tried to stress to British and US intelligence officials how useful he could be in matters of mutual interest, such as the recolonization of East Timor.

But Whitlam's insistence on talking about Pine Gap and Nurrungar in public, and his emphasis on exposing CIA plots against his Labour Party (plots which did indeed exist), sealed the politician's fate. He was dismissed by the governor-general, Sir John Kerr, in a highly unusual move that bore the imprimatur of US intelligence action. Whitlam's former defense secretary confirmed in late 2000 that Kerr met with CIA and NSA representatives on November 8, 1975, three days before the removal of the prime minister. They provided him with specific warnings of consequences to Australian interests if Whitlam was to remain in power.[4]

The irony in the NSA providing aid to CIA efforts at disrupting governments stemmed from the fact that the CIA's Office of SIGINT Operations was taking the lead in moving space-based signals satellites to multi-frequency (VHF, UHF, microwave) interception from space, after NSA researchers expressed reservations in the late 1960s that such 'hyper-spectral' analysis could be accomplished. To prove that such satellites were possible, the CIA worked with TRW Corp., the company which, in collaboration with Harris Corp., later came up with the unfurlable antenna that vastly revolutionized space signals intelligence in the 1990s. The resultant Rhyolite/Aquacade satellite was first launched in the summer of 1970. Additional launches in 1973, 1977, and 1978 allowed Rhyolite to be used in a two-satellite configuration, in which two satellites were positioned over the Horn of Africa to observe the Tyuratam ICBM tests, while two more were stationed over Borneo to monitor Soviet ICBM launches from Plesetsk.

Jeffrey Richelson cites commercial and private sources who say that Rhyolite was the first family of signals intelligence satellite to intercept private and commercial microwave traffic, as well as Soviet and Chinese military-radio transmissions. The only details known about the satellite are that it sported a dish 70 feet in diameter, aimed from a body 15 feet long, weighing some 1,540 pounds. Rhyolite was one of several projects compromised by Christopher Boyce and Daulton Lee, who were arrested in early 1977 for selling satellite secrets to the Soviet Union. Officials in the Carter administration chose to prosecute Boyce and Lee for the theft of information on a canceled frequency-hopping communication satellite called Pyramider; but the real concern, of course, was over the disclosure of Rhyolite details. Intelligence officials also were worried Boyce would provide details of the TRW Corp.'s program called Argus to develop antennas far larger than those used in Rhyolite – a precursor to its 1980s folding-antenna work. During his espionage trial in the spring of 1977, Boyce tried to reveal information on CIA manipulation of the Australian political process in 1975, but was prevented from disclosing full details on why Whitlam had been removed — to prevent a full exposure of how the NSA, the NRO, and the CIA's Office of SIGINT Operations worked together at Pine Gap.

In the final months of the Ford administration, at least four major satellite systems were initiated. The forementioned Jumpseat, controlled from Buckley Field, had its first launch from Vandenberg in March 1975. It used a highly-elliptical orbit varying from 240 miles to 24,000 miles, to perform 'close-listen' functions on targets of interest. Sharing Jumpseat's orbital pattern was the specialized Satellite Data System satellite. SDS, based on a concept devised by Bud Wheelon and perfected by CIA researchers Carl Duckett and Les Dirks, was used to provide inter-satellite links for transfer of imagery from the first digital-transmission photo satellite, the KH-11. It also kept watch for Soviet SLBM launches, relayed messages from the Air Force Satellite Control Facility in Sunnyvale, and transmitted messages to US bombers on over-the-pole missions.

The Navy got its first opportunity at dedicated ocean analysis with the initiation of the White Cloud series of satellites, the maiden launch of which took place on April 30, 1976. White Cloud used a large primary satellite and three sub-orbiting tethered micro-satellites to listen in on Soviet shipping and submarine radio traffic, from an inclined orbit 70 miles up. White Cloud relayed its information to a series of Naval Security Group ground stations called Classic Wizard, located at Diego Garcia; Guam; Adak, Alaska; Winter Harbor, Maine; and Edzell, Scotland. The primary downlink for Classic Wizard was located at Blossom Point, Maryland.

The CIA's KH-11 Crystal satellite had been a pet project of CIA Director Richard Helms, who fought for a legitimate real-time image delivery system to enhance image utility during times of crisis. The first KH-11 was launched December 19, 1976, long after Helms was gone, and its first photographs were provided to incoming President Jimmy Carter on January 21, 1977. Each satellite is 64 feet long, weighing 30,000 pounds. It flies lengthwise, in parallel to the Earth, with its primary camera looking down and scanning from side to side, which allows for multi-spectral imaging and stereoscopic image compilation. Since it does not run out of film, instead transferring digital imagery to Fort Belvoir, Virginia, it can stay in orbit longer than earlier imaging satellites, and orbits higher, at 150 to 250 miles. According to Richelson, military commanders for specific services and commands were forbidden to see KH-11 imagery, unlike KH-8 and KH-9 imagery, until William Kampiles' sale of KH-11 information to the Soviets made such segmentation unnecessary. It is interesting to note that by the mid-1990s, because of the transfer of strategic national assets to specific tactical military commands, the NRO was encouraging the transfer of intelligence information to military leaders first, or at least concurrent with its provision to civilian leaders.

Despite taking constant drubbing from military hardliners for its often hypocritical concern with human rights, the Carter administration traditionally has gotten positive accolades from those associated with agencies like the NSA and the NRO, because of the attention paid by CIA Director Stansfield Turner and NSA Director Bobby Ray Inman to the value of signals intelligence. As noted above, however, most of the advantages gleaned by the Carter White House were due to systems developed and planned during the Nixon and Ford administrations. Inman in particular, however, grasped the exploitation potential of real-time systems. With his background in tracking Soviet maritime activity as part of the Navy's hush-hush Task Force 157, Inman's interest in White Cloud/Classic Wizard was virtually a foregone conclusion.

While fans of Ronald Reagan often look back on the Carter administration as a time of inexcusable lapses and reversals in putting forth an aggressive military doctrine, it is important to remember that, with military hard-liner Zbigniew Brzezinski as national security advisor, and technical whiz-kid Harold Brown as defense secretary, the Carter team supported aggressive military posturing, and appropriate exploitation of real-time intelligence. From the early Presidential Directive 18 on 'National Security Strategy' to the PD-57 and PD-59 nuclear-weapons and communications deployment strategies during the crisis years of 1979–80, Carter set out to show the world that Robert Aldridge's claims of a blatant first-strike policy were true. If Carter had listened to the likes of Cyrus Vance and Patricia Derian, he might have taken the time to think long and hard about the way nuclear weapons were deployed and integrated into strategic policy, and about the way the new space-based intelligence tools were being applied. But at a time when hard-line friends of the United States like Nicaraguan President Somoza and the Shah of Iran were being overthrown, and the Soviets were preparing for an invasion of Afghanistan, it is no surprise that the president shifted slowly but irrevocably to the Brzezinski point of view.

Little progress was made in developing ABM or ASAT weapons during this period, not only because of a desire to stick with treaty constraints, but because tactical missiles took a back seat to intermediate-range nukes like Pershing, while lasers were facing difficult hurdles to practical applications in anti-missile roles. A few chemical and free-electron laser projects, such as the classified Sipapu program at Lawrence Livermore Laboratories, were promoted by Brown, but the Defense and Energy Departments always assumed long-term payoffs on these programs. This only enraged the conservative outsiders in the Committee on the Present Danger and High Frontier coalitions, who began making outrageous claims that Carter was 'disarming America.' The long and torturous struggle to conclude a MIRV-limiting SALT II Treaty was attacked immediately by conservative groups, and was given lukewarm support at best by many Democrats close to Carter.

One satellite system fielded at the midpoint of the administration, which aided the first-strike effort in key ways, was the Navstar satellite and the Global Positioning System it supported. While promoted to the public as an open way of determining location in three dimensions, Navstar GPS always had warfighting roots. The Transit satellite system that was Navstar's predecessor had been developed precisely for accurate targeting of submarine-launched ballistic missiles, and Navstar's primary justification was to allow first-strike counterforce accuracy for the D-5 missile in the Trident submarine, as well as for many conventional weapons in the growing US arsenal. The first prototype GPS satellites were launched in 1978, and the network was expanded to 24 satellites in six orbital planes by the mid-1990s. Controlled from a new base east of Colorado Springs, Navstar/GPS was so critical to tactical military planning efforts, that a later Defense Department program to improve its accuracy was dubbed 'Navwar.'

With the Navy background of both Turner and Inman, and the broader interest in global navigation and the White Cloud/Classic Wizard systems, it was to be expected that Navy programs in the Indian Ocean and Persian Gulf would occupy the administration's attention. The State Department had entertained talk of an Indian Ocean 'Zone of Peace' in 1977, but always placed the completion of the Diego Garcia base west of India ahead of any nuclear-free-zone discussions. In the final months of Gerald Ford's administration, Ford had been outraged at Congress's reticence to fund antenna construction on Diego Garcia, and sought Britain's help in making sure the joint British–American base could be completed on time to handle regional emergencies in South Asia. He also asked his defense secretary, James Schlesinger, to prepare an alarmist presentation for Congress on the Soviet signals and submarine base at Berbera, in hopes of freeing up funds for Diego Garcia.

Carter's efforts to juggle Horn of Africa bases became even more convoluted. Somalian dictator Siad Barre had been ready to expel the Soviets from Berbera and hand the base over to the US, but the Americans asked him to delay until Diego Garcia was finished. Carter talked Congress into approving $3.3 million in new signals funding for Diego Garcia in May 1977, claiming that the loss of a Thai signals base in U Tapao required the expansion. Barre received $450 million in advance funding from the US for the Soviet expulsion, but ended up using the money to invade Ethiopia in July. Barre expelled the Soviets in November (and the Russian Army promptly came to Ethiopia's aid), but the US refused to move any naval or NSA resources to Berbera. Instead, Carter opened three-way talks with France and Djibouti, after Djibouti declared independence in July 1977, in order to share signals intelligence resources there between US and French troops.

The relationship with French PM Valery Giscard d'Estaing proved problematic, however, because France had proposed in the UN the creation of an international monitoring agency to take on duties of the NRO and the NSA. Needless to say, the members of the UKUSA Treaty were singularly uninterested in discussing such proposals.

The collapse of the Iranian government at the end of 1978 represented the conversion of Jimmy Carter into born-again cold warrior. Carter simply could not abandon the Shah as easily as critics wished, since Iran represented a third of all US military sales worldwide. US intelligence officials were fully cognizant of the vulnerability of the Kabkan and Klarabad NSA bases in Iran, particularly after revolutionary officers seized the listening posts in February 1979, temporarily holding NSA floor agents and related civilians hostage. US officials immediately opened sensitive discussions with Chinese officials to build two listening posts in Xinjiang province, at Qitai and Korla, to replace the Iranian posts, but the administration could not tell anyone in Congress about the China deal.

Long before the embassy hostage crisis of November 1979, Carter used the Iran turmoil to justify new military alliances worldwide. In February 1979, carriers were sent to North Yemen in response to threats from South Yemen, an AWACS radar-plane deal was initiated with Saudi Arabia, and $390 million of direct aid was pledged by Carter to South Yemen, bypassing Congress. National Security Advisor Brzezinski bypassed CIA Director Turner, going directly to Deputy Director Frank Carlucci, to propose a covert program to overthrow the government of South Yemen.

Similar hardline approaches to crises in Central America and Southeast Asia all but eliminated the influence of the moderate State Department. Supporting the hard right in Nicaragua and El Salvador had little strategic effect but to undermine talk of human rights. However, the US decision to fully back China and the exile Cambodian government of Pol Pot, thereby snubbing Vietnam, was certainly a factor in Vietnam's approval of a massive Soviet signals intelligence base in Cam Ranh Bay. Meanwhile, anxiety over retaining South Korean signals and logistics bases at all costs was a motivating factor in the Carter administration's decision to fully support the May 1980 massacre of South Korean civilians involved in the Kwangju uprising.

By the time the Soviet Union invaded Afghanistan at the end of 1979, little was left of Carter's former moderate approach to bipolar relations. The first half of 1980 was spent ratcheting up the defense budget, resurrecting the draft, and publicizing first-strike nuclear policies and advanced military technology such as 'stealth' radar evasion. Of course, none of that was enough to quell the arch-conservatives behind Reagan, who blamed Carter for 'losing' Iran, Nicaragua, El Salvador, and Afghanistan (the last utterly laughable), in turn.

Carter's final victory for military and intelligence interests could not be boasted of in public. The Greek government, angry at continued Turkish intransigence over Cyprus and over Aegean Sea maneuvers, warned the US in early September 1980 that it would close NSA bases at Nea Makri and Akrotiri unless it was allowed into NATO within weeks. The civilian government in Turkey vociferously opposed this. On September 11, 1980, General Kenan Evren initiated a coup in Turkey, removing the civilian government. The Turkish military elite already had demonstrated its loyalty to the US by signing a base agreement in March 1980, which restored most NSA access to intelligence information. After the coup was consolidated, Greece was allowed back into NATO in mid-October.

This, more than any wrangling over the fate of the Iran hostages, represented the real October surprise, albeit a surprise victory for UKUSA and NATO which could never be mentioned in the US campaign. And of course, with the American people in a vengeful and ugly mood, the complex and newly-christened neo-conservative from Plains, Georgia could not hold his own against a simple movie actor who came to Washington with a dream of moving to massive military dominance on Earth, while dominating the heavens with a magical security umbrella comprised of space-based weapons.

4
Star Wars Part 2:
The Reagan Arms Buildup

When historians refer, with some fondness driven by empathy, to Ronald Reagan's nostalgic turn in the 1980s to a 'simpler America,' the most common image evoked is that of Reagan as frontier gunslinger, bringing justice to a rough world while opening new territories to a free people. Reagan's more frightening retro vision, however, was the return to a nineteenth-century model of American exceptionalism and triumphalism, evoked in his oft-used 'city on a hill' image for the isolationist state that must be made forever safe. The naïveté of this image as applied to missile defense, seeing space-based weapons as providing an impenetrable security umbrella to the domestic population, was foolhardy enough that it failed to gain initial support in 1981–82 of many within the Defense Department, including Defense Secretary Caspar Weinberger. It also served as justification for turning deterrence into crusader rollback actions, as continuously seen during the Reagan years in Latin America and Africa. This shift in national consciousness was to have lasting effect beyond the Cold War, surviving in nascent form throughout the Clinton years, and emerging virulently in the second Bush administration.

Ronald Reagan's inaugural team invaded Washington in the winter of 1981 with ambitious goals of a revolution to decentralize the domestic economy and re-establish ultra-rightist rollback schemes on the international front that would 'make America strong again.' If any further indication of the inherent hypocrisy in the dual mission was necessary, an excellent example was provided at the spectacle of the inaugural ball: ostentatiousness and concern for the rich ruled the evening, yet invitations were extended to international vermin from Europe and Latin America who literally worshipped the works of Hitler and Mussolini. Guests of honor included Mario Sandoval Alarcon and many of his associates in the Guatemalan Movement of

National Liberation, the overtly fascist organization that called itself the 'party of organized violence.' One might give the same title to the group that took over the Republican Party in the United States during the early days of the Reagan Revolution, and in fact, the wing that continued to define the Republicans through the early twenty-first century.

Given the gut-level needs of many Americans to find an enemy and lash back at the perceived sources of 1980s problems, it was not surprising to acknowledge the popularity of much of the Reagan message, despite its lunatic nature. What is tragic, however, is the number of otherwise intelligent centrists of both parties who saw political gains to be made from joining the revolution. Maniacal defense budget priorities were set, implausible political theories were promoted as doctrine within the intelligence community, and inherently unworkable covert actions were touted for political purposes. The bulk of Washington went along with only nominal protests.

The mission of 're-arming America' served as an excellent example. In reality the $200 billion in accelerated programs sought by Reagan did not amount to much more than the MX and Trident plans already put in place by Carter. But the attitude matching the expansion, such as the insistence on going ahead with Pershing II and cruise missile deployments in Europe, was enough to sour relations with the Soviet Union throughout Reagan's first term. Revisionists might say that it was precisely the 'in-your-face' chutzpah of Reagan officials that eventually led to the Soviet Union's downfall and a perceived US victory in the Cold War, but the massive numbers turning out in anti-nuclear rallies in the US and Europe in the early 1980s indicates that many citizens were frightened of such brinksmanship.

Because Reagan's March 1983 Star Wars speech was made at approximately the same time that the Air Force Space Command (AFSC) was created (the first of multiple service-specific commands, to be followed by a national US Space Command), some Star Wars critics assumed that there was a coherent US plan for weaponizing space, brought to Washington in fully-baked form by Reagan and Weinberger. This certainly was the assumption adopted by Soviet Premiers Yuri Andropov and Konstantin Chernenko, when they pushed in the 1980s for an end to weaponizing space. In reality, the bureaucrats in the NRO and Air Force Space and Missile Systems Center were following evolutionary plans to streamline management of communications, intelligence, and navigational satellites, dating from Carter's term.

The concept for a multi-tiered missile defense topped with an X-ray laser powered by H-bombs, came out of a realm of Department of Energy think-tanking that was so far afield, Defense Department officials were not sure how to respond to Reagan's March 1983 Strategic Defense Initiative (SDI) proposal for nearly two years. Exoatmospheric interceptor rockets, though they could be made smaller in principle than Nike-era systems due to the emergence of very large-scale chip integration for missile electronics, were not much more reliable than systems of the late 1960s. Air- and space-based laser systems were perceived by most in the military and private industry to be decades from practical application.

Two days after the March 1983 speech, Reagan issued a National Security Decision Directive that eventually led to establishment of the Strategic Defense Initiative Office in early 1984, headed by Lt. Gen. James Abrahamson. A presidential commission under James Fletcher published a classified report advocating a five-tier missile defense regime, including directed-energy and space-based weapons that could stop missiles in boost-phase; air-based lasers and 'smart rocks' that could stop warheads in midcourse phase; and ground-based kinetic-kill weapons capable of stopping warheads in terminal phase. Yet despite all the activity, virtually no publicity was given to SDI between the president's speech and the beginning of his second term.

There was a very good reason for this. Weinberger, Abrahamson, and DARPA Director Robert Cooper supported SDI as a means of protecting US *missiles*, thereby enhancing a potential first strike. As a means of protecting *populations*, Star Wars technologies would not be ready in years, or even decades, to achieve the level of effectiveness necessary for stopping all warheads launched by a state with advanced MIRV technology. If one assumed that the primary adversary was a superpower with MIRVs, like the Soviet Union or even China, and if one assumed that no arms control initiatives with the Soviet Union were forthcoming, then SDI could only be seen as a first-strike enhancer, not as a population-protector. In her definitive study of Reagan administration nuclear and SDI strategy, *Way Out There In The Blue*, Frances FitzGerald claims that there was nothing covert about this policy, but neither was there much of an effort to explain it adequately to the American people. 'Administration experts,' she wrote, 'might seem to be arguing the feasibility of population defenses, but in reality they were doing no such thing – at least not in the company of knowledgeable people.'[1]

What would be surprising, were it not for the overall intransigence and first-strike orientation of Weinberger, was how tightly the administration clung to a demand that it could move SDI weapons from research labs to the field, despite the rudimentary state of many development programs. The only experiments that seemed to carry hope later were shown to have been manipulated, such as the Homing Overlay Experiment of 1984. Even assuming that the Reagan–Gorbachev October 1986 Reykjavik summit involved some unrealistic grandstanding proposals by Gorbachev for the full elimination of nuclear weapons, Reagan was absolutely intransigent on SDI issues where he need not have been. SDI weapons on any tier were not ready for prime time, and still were not by 2003.

The Air Force's plans for management of the space battlefield, meanwhile, had little to do with arcane strategic policy, and everything to do with making multiple networks work together. While Air Force Space Command was born with a mission of 'space control,' it did not initially adopt the rhetoric in the broader form seen in the post-Cold War period. Space surveillance and missile warning duties were shifted in the late 1970s from Aerospace Defense Command to Strategic Command, but the move was seen by most in the Air Force and the Pentagon at large as singularly unsuccessful. In February 1979, a Space Missions Study was commissioned within the Air Force, which worked through the presidential transition period. In August 1981, Gen. James Hartinger of the Aerospace Defense Command met with Gen. Robert Marsh of Air Force Systems Command to decide on dedicated space operations, based on one of the options suggested in the study. After taking some initial ideas to a group of generals meeting as the 'Corona' team, Air Force Chief of Staff Lew Allen approved of an Air Force Space Command in June 1982, and the command was officially commissioned at Peterson Air Force Base in September 1982.

The command immediately took responsibility for all major terrestrial space observation systems, including the new Ground-Based Electro-Optical Deep Space Surveillance telescopes being built in Socorro, New Mexico; Maui, Hawaii; Chae Jong-San, South Korea; and Diego Garcia. It also took control of a new Pacific Barrier Radar System, or PACBAR, which had ground stations at Kwajalein, the Philippines, and Saipan.

In May 1983, a Consolidated Space Operations Center was designated for space-control operations at the new Falcon Air Force Station east of Colorado Springs, and by September 1985 the CSOC was open, controlling GPS, DSCS, DSP, Milstar, and Defense Meteorological Satellite Program systems. The CSOC was touted in public as primarily a base to control military operations of the space shuttle, but that was always a tangential mission, making its 'reorganization' after the 1986 *Challenger* disaster less of an issue than was perceived. Because of the expanded role of Falcon (later Schriever) and Peterson Air Force Bases in controlling space missions worldwide, a special multi-service US Space Command was established at Peterson in September 1985.

In its very early days, the Reagan administration had aimed for a certain level of detached professionalism in its intelligence agencies. Bobby Ray Inman was moved from the NSA to the CIA, where he pledged to play a professional and straight role as deputy director under Bill Casey. Gen. Lincoln Faurer became NSA director, where he managed to keep the NSA segregated from some of the more hare-brained schemes launched in Reagan's early years.

Inman did not last long because of the inherent struggles between the 'Atlanticists' and the 'cowboys.' The former were supporters of the UKUSA Treaty behind Secretary of State Alexander Haig, who wanted to provide unfettered support to Britain in its war in the Falklands, and Israel in its invasion of Lebanon. The cowboys, led by National Security Advisor William Clark and CIA Director Casey, were willing to sacrifice some elements of European support in order to more fully back the Argentine government in the Falklands to reward it for its support of the *contras* in Nicaragua. Inman was particularly uncomfortable over the way in which selective monitoring was used, but then kept segmented, when Israel bombed the Osirak reactor in Iraq in July 1981. He was also upset with several

instances in which Haig misrepresented CIA and NSA information in order to provide more support for an aggressive position
in El Salvador and Nicaragua. While Inman was short-lived, Haig
also did not survive the twin crises of 1982, the Falklands and
Lebanon, since he was seen as too singularly supportive of Britain
and Israel.

Because Haig was clearly the most arrogant on the Reagan staff,
some might have thought that his departure would mean a more
nuanced and careful security staff. Instead, all that happened was
that the proponents of global rollback reigned supreme. The new
Secretary of State George Shultz was more moderate in some
senses than Haig, but he also routinely lost battles on issues of
CIA misadventures in Central America.

Until military exercises in Central America ramped up in early
1983, and US Marines were deployed to Beirut at the same time,
the US government played a secondary support role in the first
global crises of the Reagan era. Occasionally, the US military
would take on a direct battle role, such as in the shootdown of
Libyan planes over the Gulf of Sidra during the Libya–Chad
battles, but for the most part, the US was providing intelligence
support to other nations on the front line.

Space-based intelligence resources were not nearly as coordinated as they would be in the Gulf War of 1991 (which itself was
an amateurish prelude to how space would be used in the war
on terror). Nevertheless, NSA and NRO resources were exploited
to an extent never before seen in the agencies' histories, in
tracking long and festering crises in Poland and Central America,
as well as shorter, more traditional skirmishes in the Falklands
and Lebanon. This meant unprecedented collection of signals
intelligence that needed to be stored and archived, and unprecedented strain on the 'floor agents' that served as electronics
technicians, linguists, and cryptanalysts at NSA ground stations.
One Army Security Agency source who worked at the Gablingen
'elephant cage,' listening to Polish traffic in the period between
the threatened Soviet invasion of December 1980 and the declaration of martial law a year later, said that stress levels were so
high that drug use was rampant at Gablingen, and nervous
breakdowns were common. One message that Faurer consistently
provided to the White House was that, if tactical monitoring of
every single global hot spot was going to expand exponentially,

the NSA needed more resources, better strategies for storing information, and better means of distributing that information to the field. Despite traditional inter-agency rivalries, the NSA and the NRO began to increase plans to move more resources to space, something long sought in the Nixon, Ford, and Carter eras to cut down on NSA floor-station vulnerability.

At some point early in the Reagan administration, TRW and Harris Corp. made presentations to the NRO and Air Force on new concepts of folding antennas, capable of picking up HF, VHF, and UHF traffic. The antennas could be curled up in a helix type of configuration to fit within the confines of the fairing of large space vehicles. The specs provided for such antennas helped drive the requirements for a special adjunct to the space shuttle called the Inertial Upper Stage, as well as for payloads for the gargantuan Titan-IV rocket. Design plans for these antennas called for future systems in which antennas could expand in space to the length of three football fields. Full details of such systems remain some of the most classified US government technologies in existence.

On the ground, the successful pursuit of the aggressive form of 'low-intensity warfare' favored by Reagan required a subtle balance between the all-out commitment of antenna bases and radio-research teams used in Vietnam, and the semi-automated listening posts developed under La Faire Vite that were replacing heavily-populated snooping stations at key locations. Signals intelligence resources in the Army Intelligence Support Activity (ISA) and the Navy Seaspray operation provided mobility, high technology, and deniability for many Central American actions, but the Pentagon of the 1980s still was a long way from the space-supported battle groups of the early twenty-first century.

Direct intelligence support in Central American actions was routine well before the massive Big Pine I and II operations in Honduras in 1983. The Army Intelligence and Security Command had run the Royal Duke signals intelligence flights out of Honduras and El Salvador since the start of the Reagan administration. NSA had set up a multi-service listening post on Tiger Island, where Nicaragua, Honduras, and El Salvador came together. The ISA and NSA were running a series of highly secret intelligence flights, using private planes, in operations called Queens Hunter and Graphic Book. Support for the contras, whether run by the CIA or private armies, became almost inconsequential compared to the total US intelligence dominance of the battlefield.

For its begrudging deployment to Lebanon, the United States had to rely on many more Israeli resources, despite the reticence even the hard-bitten members of the Reagan administration had for working with the Israeli Aman intelligence agency following the massacres at Sabra and Shatila in late 1982. Every time the US tried to send regional intelligence specialists to the area, they would be targeted almost immediately by Hezbollah or other Islamic factions. Photographic and signals intelligence satellites were continuously repositioned for use over the Middle East, yet US officials were well aware that they could only gain true situational awareness in areas in which they could exert uncontested physical control.

European allies were proving more of a hindrance than a help in the 1982–83 period, when a sudden wave of 'bases flu' swept the continent, driven in part by a legitimate moral shock at the aggressive tones of the Reagan administration, and in part by a desire to eke more money out of the Reagan-era defense buildup. Greece, under a new socialist administration that was bitter about the ongoing Cyprus crisis, threatened once again to shut down Nea Makri and Iraklion, before agreeing to a five-year extension to its basing pact in exchange for a $500 million payment. Portugal pushed hard for more than $100 million to keep the Lajes air field in the Azores open. And Felipe Gonzales' government in Spain threatened to close air bases at Rota and Torrejon, before agreeing to a pact that would keep them open until the 1990s.

Add to this uncertainty the new doubts about Britain engendered by the revelations of the damage that GCHQ spy Geoffrey Prime had done to expose NSA expansions at Menwith Hill and Oakhangar, and the elements were in place for an NRO/NSA move to space.

Given the overwhelming popularity of Reagan's landslide victory in 1984, it is easy to forget how frightened the world community was in the latter half of 1983, before a new regime came into place in Moscow. In rapid succession, the US cut off many ties with the Soviet Union following the Russian shootdown of Korean Air Lines Flight 007 on August 31, 1983;

the US invaded the tiny island nation of Grenada for no clear
reason other than to show the flag; the American military communications test Able Archer 83 was interpreted as a possible
nuclear attack by the Kremlin; and the first Pershing II missiles
arriving in Germany in November caused the Soviets to walk out
on virtually any practical arms discussions with the United
States. It seems shocking in retrospect that few Americans could
understand how aggressive they were perceived even by many
allies, let alone the Soviet Union.

Even the worst Soviet errors carried hints of American provo-
cations and abuses. In the case of KAL007, for example, the
evidence may be far from clear that the commercial flight was
serving a direct intelligence purpose, yet writers Seymour Hersh
and Duncan Campbell both have made convincing cases that US
intelligence agencies used the particular flight plan of KAL007 to
gain maximum intelligence information through Cobra Ball and
Rivet Joint intelligence flights from Alaska, and through a Ferret
signals intelligence satellite launched concurrently with a KH-9,
which synchronized with the KAL007 flight plan. Only a few
Reagan officials like Richard Perle (who would later show up in
the George W. Bush administration) were brash enough to
espouse a 'we own the world' propaganda line in the early 1980s,
but the imperial overreach of the Reagan administration set the
stage for what the younger George Bush would do 20 years later.

With historical distance, many students of the Reagan era
would like to believe that the president softened his hard line in
response to the multiple arms initiatives promoted by Mikhail
Gorbachev in the Soviet Union. Given the cloud under which
covert operators were living in 1986–87 with the revelations of
Iran-contra, it would make sense to think that belligerence had
taken a back seat to practical dialogue. But the truth of the matter
is that the last three years of the Reagan administration represented the worst period of intransigence for US positions
emphasizing rollback and empire-building. Sadly, Democrats in
Congress often took harder-line positions than members of the
Reagan administration, in matters such as provision of Stinger
missiles to the Afghanistan mujahedeen. The days of the Boland
amendment, which forced *contra* financing into the private
networks run by Oliver North, were forgotten in the late 1980s
atmosphere in which the *contras* in Nicaragua and bordering

countries received $100 million and the Afghan rebels $300 million, all with the open blessing of both parties in Congress.

In retrospect, it is all too apparent where the Space Command picked up its 'we own the planet' language, since that assumption was implicit in most of the activities of US ground-based and naval services. The US Navy in particular, under the guidance of John Lehman and Adm. William Crowe, went to lengths that even the grand strategists of the Eisenhower and Nixon eras would not have attempted. In particular, the brash activities of the US intelligence ship *Caron* in the first half of 1986, which included direct penetration of seas surrounding the Crimean peninsula and the ramming of Soviet vessels, would have sparked a possible nuclear alert in the time of Brezhnev. Only Gorbachev's wish to seek greater stability in superpower relations allowed the US Navy to get away with some of its outrageous activity in the Black Sea.

The Navy also set in place new relations in the Persian Gulf, which allowed the US to take a domineering role in the 're-flagging' sea battles of 1987, in the waning days of the Iran–Iraq war. In Bahrain, a berthing island used by the Sixth Fleet since the late 1970s was upgraded with antenna fields and forward-projection capabilities in the mid-1980s. The United States took over a GCHQ antenna field at Masirah in Oman as the British relation with Oman cooled, and the Naval Security Group contracted with Tetra Tech International to build a second naval intelligence facility at Masandam in Oman. Israel made half-hearted efforts to get the US to reopen the Kagnew listening post in Ethiopia, since it had entertained overtures from Dergue leader Mengistu Haile Mariam, but the US would not forgive the torturing of a CIA agent by Dergue officials in the mid-1980s, and the efforts came to naught.

The Navy, backed up by space agencies, took a particularly aggressive role in the South Pacific in the mid-1980s, centered primarily on New Zealand Prime Minister David Lange's 'nuclear flu,' and the cutoff of intelligence sharing that resulted from Lange's refusal to allow nuclear-armed ships to berth in New Zealand. Authors such as Desmond Ball and Nicky Hager have demonstrated that the so-called intelligence cutoff affected primarily civilians in New Zealand, not the relations between the NSA and the New Zealand Government Communications

Security Bureau. But the hard line in the Pacific involved far more than New Zealand.

US officials demanded that all trust territories sign 'Compacts of Free Association,' which would trade some political and trade autonomy in exchange for open-ended rights of the US to maintain bases and weapons tests. When Kwajalein renounced its compact in 1982 (an action that had no effect on the operation of the missile-defense facility there), the Pentagon insisted on taking a hard line in similar cases. The Palau (Belau) independence movement, for example, not only had to face harsh language from State and Defense Department officials in the mid-1980s, but two Palau independence leaders were assassinated under mysterious circumstances in 1985 and 1988. The US provided the French military with some indirect signals help in quelling an uprising in New Caledonia, and may have provided some indirect assistance to the group that bombed Greenpeace's *Rainbow Warrior*. Still undetermined is the official US and French role in the 1987 coup in Fiji. In all cases, however, allied agencies were trying to protect space and nuclear facilities from threats from independence movements. This is why even a civilian leader of a primary UKUSA nation like New Zealand could be undermined in the atmosphere the Reagan team promoted in the mid-1980s. Anyone who questioned a single element of the US forward-basing nuclear strategy was deemed suspect.

In retrospect, the profound changes promoted by Mikhail Gorbachev in the Soviet Union should have led to immediate changes in the attitudes of both the Reagan hard-core team, and the incoming Bush team that employed several Reagan rightists. It is true that, following the final collapse of the Soviet Union, Bush was willing to initiate a level of arms-reduction planning which Bill Clinton later failed to capitalize on. But this change of heart only took place after several years' worth of space and intelligence expansion by the US, funded even after the Soviet Union began its economic and political decline. By the second Reagan term, intelligence planning had turned to a real-time, 24-hour unilateral delivery system that fulfilled tactical as well as strategic goals, and space already was being touted as a realm that should fall under sole US control.

5
Intelligence Goes Real-Time

The value of digitizing imaging information had been apparent since a special US intelligence committee, convened in the aftermath of the 1967 Six-Day War, gave birth to the KH-11 satellite. Not only would digital transmission of images allow near-real-time delivery of time-sensitive data, but digital images could be filtered at will to emphasize particular frequency bands, something not possible with analog film spools.

The NRO and the NSA took slightly longer to reach an equivalent conclusion for signals intelligence, though not because they failed to recognize the limits or hazards inherent in ground-based listening posts. The casualties experienced in many foreign NSA outposts had been one of the drivers for moving to remotely-operated bases, first realized on the European front line in La Faire Vite, and later expanded in region-specific NSA programs such as Explorer and Guardrail. But the migration from the Chalet to Vortex class of microwave-only satellite, like the migration from Rhyolite to Magnum in the multi-frequency arena, proved far more difficult than anticipated. Not only did the NRO and the NSA have to jointly request classified line items several times larger than any space item to date (with some satellites approaching $1 billion each), but dedicated launch subsystems had to be employed for the new monstrous birds.

The Inertial Upper Stage, designed by Boeing, was intended as a temporary stand-in for a planned space 'tugboat' that fell victim to budget cuts. Originally, IUS was supposed to be used in conjunction with either the space shuttle, a modified Titan III, or the massive Titan IV rocket. The 17-foot x 9.25-foot solid-fuel rocket subsystem was intended to carry loads as large as 5,000 pounds up to geosynchronous orbit, after the shuttle or a Titan IV had taken IUS to a lower orbit. The first two IUS systems, for DSCS-2 and DSCS-3 satellites, were lofted on a Titan III in October 1982. NASA launched its Tracking and Data Relay Satellite (which, incidentally, was used to support many classified Air Force missions), using the IUS on the shuttle's STS-6 mission in April 1983.

Finally, the first NSA Magnum satellite was carried to geosynchronous orbit by an IUS inside the bay of the first fully military shuttle mission, STS-51C in January 1985, a mission which had virtually every aspect of its flight classified. Magnum was unique in being the first UKUSA 'time-shared' satellite – when the British government decided it could not afford its own Zircon signals intelligence satellite, the US government agreed to lease time on the Magnum satellite, which featured a 160-foot antenna.

On the ground, additional space-support stations were required to provide redundant downlinks for some government satellites, and to provide secret ground-based intercept posts to pick up communications from Intelsat satellites. In its early days, the NSA had been interested primarily in military communications, though the original focus on the Soviet Union and China had expanded in the 1960s to cover developing nations and industrial allies alike. By the end of that decade, the UKUSA nations were listening in on all military forces worldwide.

As a result of the decades-old Shamrock and Minaret operations to intercept communications in the domestic US, the NSA also recognized the value in snooping on civilian communications, in the form of commercial traffic as well as the individual communications of civilian targets of interest. While the NSA promised in Congressional hearings in the mid-1970s to end the interception of private communications of US citizens within US borders, it made no such promises for the communications of any person outside the US, or of any US citizen communicating with someone in another nation. In addition, the NSA reserved the right to perform broadband 'testing,' in which communications would be intercepted in bulk, even within US borders. The vacuum-cleaner type of interception performed at so-called test facilities in locations such as San Angelo, Texas and Fort Huachuca, Arizona, effectively bypassed any promises the NSA made to Congress on domestic interception.

But by the late 1970s, most of the interesting commercial traffic no longer moved through microwave relays, where it could be intercepted through high-frequency antenna systems. It would still be a few years before transatlantic fiber-optic cables took on the bulk of international phone transmission, but Intelsat was doing a good job of filling the gap. Consequently, the satellite system became a key target for the NSA.

For the first widely-used generation of Intelsat satellite, Intelsat-4, the UKUSA alliance relied on NSA's Yakima Field Station in eastern Washington state, the Misawa Air Force Security Service base in Japan, new dishes at the existing Sabana Seca site in Puerto Rico, and GCHQ's Morwenstow base near Bude in England. Some sites appeared to be chosen for their earlier participation in an NSA intercept program called Ladylove, involved in listening in on the Soviet *Gorizont* and *Raduga* communication satellites. In addition to the Misawa and Yakima bases, NSA sites in Guam, and in Rosman, North Carolina were used for Ladylove. (Rosman was turned over to the US Forest Service in 1995, perhaps because its secrecy had been compromised.)

As the commercial Intelsat network evolved to Intelsat-4A and Intelsat-5 in the early 1980s, NSA reopened a former Naval Research Labs facility at Sugar Grove, Virginia. GCHQ, meanwhile, used a remotely-operated facility in Chum Hom Kok, Hong Kong, that was managed by a joint group of Australian and New Zealand officials in Melbourne. (Hong Kong interception duties later were transferred to Shoal Bay, Australia, following China's takeover of the island.) When Intelsat moved to the Intelsat-7 series in 1994, additional interception stations were opened in Geraldton, Australia; Waihopai, New Zealand; and probably on the South Atlantic island of Ascension, where the NSA and GCHQ already maintained multi-purpose antenna facilities near the community of Two Boats.[1]

Executives with Intelsat and other international carriers have expressed some frustration in the early twenty-first century, not at the interception program itself, but at not being offered exclusive deals with the NRO or the National Imagery and Mapping Agency (NIMA), in the way that commercial imaging companies have struck deals for image supply during times of war. Inmarsat, Intelsat, and other carriers insist they would be willing to launch satellites with dedicated payloads for the Pentagon, provided they could get some advance money, or concepts for specifications, from the US government. (Such desire to be 'good corporate citizens' during the post-September 11 period may explain the context of why Western Union and AT&T agreed to help the NSA intercept telegrams in Project Shamrock during the early years of the Cold War.) The Bush

White House, however, rejected all such offers in 2003, insisting that communication carriers were not as 'strategic' as commercial imaging satellite services. Meanwhile, satellite carriers do their best to avoid all mention or complaints over interception programs aimed specifically at their satellites.[2]

As the construction of Intelsat interception stations moved into full swing during the Reagan administration, a massive expansion of interpretive computer systems, linked to regional intelligence bases, was designed and deployed under Lincoln Faurer and William Odom at the NSA. The architecture of the global network was called Platform or P-415, but civil liberties advocates in the 1990s referred to this expanded UKUSA commercial-traffic interception program by the name of its keyword-search system: Echelon. Centralized NSA facilities at Fort Meade and key SIGINT regional centers had large vector-processing supercomputers of the Cray or Floating Point Systems class, or occasionally massively-parallel supercomputers from Thinking Machines Inc., Silicon Graphics Inc., or Intel Corp. But the Echelon processing centers and RSOCs (Regional SIGINT Operation Centers) relied on simpler combinations of Digital Equipment Corp. VAXes, Tandem Computer fault-tolerant computers running the Non-Stop operating system, and Compaq Computer Corp. servers for general-purpose input–output (by the 1990s, all three architectures were owned by Compaq, a company later acquired by Hewlett-Packard).

The computers and the databases they relied upon for keyword searches were called Dictionary, while the overall topology and architecture of keyword-search intelligence was called Echelon. Nicky Hager, in his authoritative 1996 book *Secret Power*, provided the most detailed descriptions of how allies in the UKUSA network would make the Dictionary system work for the maximum advantage of all agencies in the network.

At certain critical terrestrial bases, simultaneous construction projects were initiated to support the interception of commercial communication satellite traffic, as well as to support ground processing for the concurrent Magnum/Orion upgrades to Rhyolite, and the Vortex/Mercury upgrades to Chalet. British journalist Duncan Campbell expanded his probe of Menwith Hill in the late 1980s, and was aided by a broadened protest campaign against the base that turned to widely-publicized civil disobedience. While demonstrations sponsored by Greenpeace and the Campaign for Nuclear Disarmament were a regular feature at Menwith Hill in the 1980s, a women's encampment, involving several veterans of the Greenham Common campaign, began a camp-out at Menwith Hill in the early 1990s. A regular series of base 'raids' garnered the women some information on base expansion, which they shared with Campbell and other journalists. WoMenwith Hill campaigners Anne Lee and Helen John also turned up critical information on the fiber-optic cables British Telecom maintained between Menwith Hill, and the nearby BT microwave-relay site at Hunters Stones. Meanwhile, Lindis Percy and Anni Rainbow of the Campaign for the Accountability of American Bases maintained separate actions against other US signals and communications bases in the area, expanding independent awareness of US/UK military space activity in Yorkshire and the Leeds–Harrogate area.

Campbell and the women of Menwith Hill assembled information showing that the expansions included the SILKWORTH program for long-range radio monitoring; the MOONPENNY program for monitoring satellite communications; RUNWAY, to control Chalet and Vortex, and STEEPLEBUSH I and II, a separate facility for controlling Magnum/Orion satellites.[3]

In the early 1990s, Colorado activists affiliated with Citizens for Peace in Space and other organizations began a similar campaign to raise awareness on Buckley and Schriever air bases. While documents of the level of Menwith Hill detail were never uncovered for Buckley, a military-construction notice for the Colorado base showed a priority level of DX BRICKBAT, normally reserved only for strategic nuclear construction projects. In addition to expansions related to the signals intelligence satellites, three new radomes at the far southeast corner of the base were linked by Campbell to an update of the Navy White Cloud program called RANGER. In a second wave of expansion, massive intelligence-processing facilities were built outside Buckley, under the control of private contractors, including Raytheon and Lockheed-Martin. Where the British women could make numerous forays into Menwith Hill with minimal legal effects, Colorado activists attempting to approach the Aerospace Data Facility area of Buckley regularly were tackled and dragged to jail, while photographers had film confiscated. CPIS Director

Bill Sulzman had some luck in getting one daily newspaper and the local business press interested in the story, but most members of the Colorado media were frightened to probe the Denver area's largest employer too deeply. Colorado members of Congress active on the intelligence committees wanted nothing to do with looking into the Buckley expansion.[4]

The similar expansions at Bad Aibling in Germany were noted only by intelligence analyst Erich Schmidt-Eenboom, until a cover *Der Speigel* story in the spring of 1997 finally exposed Bad Aibling's role as a signals intelligence station. Bad Aibling was slated for phase-out early in the twenty-first century, though following the terror attacks of September 11, such plans were postponed indefinitely. But Schmidt-Eenboom told reporters in Europe that it has been an uphill struggle to get German peace or environmental groups to grasp Bad Aibling's connections to space warfare, or to the civil liberties violations inherent in Echelon.

Unlike earlier programs based on custom equipment, the Echelon, Vortex, and Magnum expansions of the late 1980s and early 1990s were based largely on commercial off-the-shelf equipment from Digital Equipment Corp., Tandem, Compaq Computer, and other computer companies. While the NSA was willing to contract with commercial computer companies for both supercomputing codebreaker systems and client/server keyword-search computers, the agency wanted to retain control over security methodologies, as well as the basic digital logic chips (microprocessors, communication processors, and digital signal processors) used in designing the most sensitive of internal systems. By the mid-1980s, the NSA had taken over most computer security standards development for the computer industry at large, and its authoritative 'rainbow' books (Orange Book, Blue Book, etc.) of computer security standards were accepted not only as a guide in designing for federal acquisition processes, but as a guide for designing secure systems in the commercial world. At the end of the 1980s, NSA officials attended several semiconductor industry events warning of a Japanese takeover of the industry (a threat which failed to materialize in any field save DRAM memories), and finally contracted with National Semiconductor Corp. to set up a classified chip-design center and semiconductor wafer fabrication plant, located at NSA headquarters at Fort Meade, Maryland. By the end of the

1990s, the chip facility was looking for outside work to stretch federal dollars, and the NSA Microelectronics Center began advertising its design capabilities openly at industry conferences.

The weakest link in the technical intelligence community's overall plans lay in the shift of phone calls carried by satellite or microwave link to optical fibers and advanced wireless networks, as well as the shift from circuit-switched analog calls to communications based on packet-switched, connectionless links between sender and receiver. On the optical front, it was not completely true that an optical fiber could not be tapped. If optical test equipment was placed at certain critical points in packet-switched networks, packets of interests could be copied and analyzed. But this was not an easy task, and the NSA poured money into an early 1990s program called MONET (Multiple Wavelength Optical Network) to try and influence how equipment of the future, such as Optical Add-Drop Multiplexers and Dense Wave Division Multiplexers, would be designed. By the early twenty-first century, the slow pace of optical snooping had led to a special $282 million contract which the NSA provided to Science Applications International Corp., part of the NSA Project Trailblazer, to find new ways to intercept communications carried in the ether and over optical fiber.

For wireless calls, first-generation analog cellular calls carried at 800 MHz were not too difficult to intercept, once they were aggregated at metropolitan switching centers. But as cellular networks turned to packet switching in the 1990s, the NSA and the FBI both found it difficult to catch up. When signals traveled through the air in a cellular or microcellular infrastructure in urban areas, they could be intercepted from ground stations, though the strength of the radiated power did not allow effective interception from space. Once cellular calls went from the base-station controller to the metropolitan switching center, they entered the same common public-switched telephone network that carried land-line calls. These calls could be intercepted when they were relayed in aggregate over microwave towers, but that became less and less common as the optical backbone lines reached a condition of over-capacity in the late 1990s. Hence, agencies such as the NSA and the NRO could provide help to low-earth orbit communication companies that would hopefully provide payback later, while at the same time encouraging an infrastructure that was easier to intercept. The agencies' indirect involvement in space-based wireless communication networks owned by commercial consortia, such as Iridium and Globalstar, held out the hope that such networks might be easier to monitor. But the low-earth orbit communication networks never proved to be economical compared to the terrestrial digital cellular networks spreading worldwide.

A fringe benefit of the rapid growth of terrestrial cellular networks, not widely recognized until the early twenty-first century, was the ability to use a distributed network of signals as an active-radar source for target location and, potentially at least, in snooping duties. In early 2003, British research firm Roke Manor Research LLC announced a contract with BAe Systems to develop a search radar receiver called Celldar, which would take advantage of distributed microwave emanations from cellular phone towers. Roke Manor was reported to be exploring parallel vector search algorithms, to be able to use cellular network signals in radar search tasks, with the consent of neither wireless operators, nor cellular users. The effort underscored the common set of problems and technologies shared by the radar and signals-intelligence communities.[5]

As communication shifted from nailed-up phone calls to packet communications based on Internet Protocol packets, the new technology of packet switching provided a new type of headache for the Pentagon and domestic law enforcement in the US. The intelligence community had its own series of Internet-like classified networks, including IntelNet and SIPRNET (Secret IP Router Network), but the packet communications used by the Internet were profoundly different from the circuit-based com-munications of the past. Traditional phone calls involved a direct, nailed-up connection established between sender and receiver. In an Internet e-mail, or a 'Voice Over Internet Protocol' voice call, messages are broken up into packets and each packet can be sent to a destination via an independent route. The FBI was the first agency to complain in public about the problem of monitoring the Internet. The agency demanded in 1994 that Congress pass the Digital Telephony Act, later known as the Communication Assistance to Law Enforcement Act, or CALEA. This basically required traditional telephony carriers and Internet Service Providers to make sure their packet networks were 'tappable.' The NSA, which already had positioned special equipment near the primary Internet nodes known as Network Access Points (NAPs) and Metropolitan Area Exchanges (MAEs), was only too happy to provide assistance to communication carriers. Of course, with the explosion of Internet traffic soon escalating exponentially over voice traffic, the NSA's traditional problem of storing, analyzing, and making sense of all the information it could collect grew far worse than it had been in the 1970s and 1980s. While the opportunity existed in theory for intercepting every voice call, every e-mail message worldwide, the US intelligence community's ability to make sense of its vast store of information was dwindling.

Nevertheless, the elements were in place for utilizing strategic intelligence in global low-intensity conflict struggles, and in support of interception of commercial traffic. But many officers within the intelligence agencies, and within the Joint Chiefs of Staff, resisted this move while the Soviet Union remained a competitive power to be reckoned with. By the time Mikhail Gorbachev assumed control of the Communist Party in the Soviet Union, virtually everyone in Washington (save for the occasional paranoid outburst from Weinberger or Senator Dan Quayle) accepted the waning of the Cold War. But it would take the combined impact of the Gulf War and the Soviet Union's collapse to finally allow the global intelligence take of the NSA and the NRO to be utilized for maximum advantage by the new space-based military bureaucracy.

Those suspicious of centralized government intelligence capabilities tend to forget that bureaucracies often can hinder the ability of multiple agencies to share data. The regional conflicts supported in part by US intelligence agencies in the 1980s certainly were covered and influenced by signals intelligence, and particularly space-based communications and intelligence, more than in decades past. But tactical commanders rarely could gain access to information that combined sources from the three military services, as well as national intelligence agencies. The Gulf War often is cited as the first conflict to take advantage of such cross-disciplinary tools, but the way in which systems such as DSP and GPS were used was still rudimentary, astonishingly so at times. Well after Desert Storm and into the early years of the Clinton administration, regional commanders still were complaining about the 'stovepipe' nature of intelligence distribution. It would take the post-Cold War rhetoric of Space Command, pushing the notion of a unified global intelligence product, to disrupt the interservice rivalries. But first, Space Command and the NRO had some growing up to do.

6
Military Space Policy, Post-*Challenger*

The Air Force had never been thrilled about its reliance on NASA's space shuttle for heavier lift missions, so the explosion of *Challenger* soon after launch in January 1986 led to a scramble within Space Command and the NRO to make sure that national-security flights, both intelligence and communications related, could be transferred to the Titan IV or smaller vehicles. Edward Cleveland 'Pete' Aldridge, director of the NRO in 1983–86, who later went on to be Secretary of the Air Force in Reagan's final two years in office, was ideally situated to determine the pros and cons of the shuttle. He had worked with the contractors for geo-synchronous spy satellites on modifying their designs to fit IUS constraints within the shuttle bay. On a more personal level, Aldridge had trained to be a mission specialist for a future shuttle mission, which came to naught after the shuttles were grounded following the *Challenger* explosion.

The new classes of massive signals intelligence satellites, both the Chalet/Vortex series and the multi-frequency Magnum series, were moving into a period of semi-regular production, without realizing significant cost advantages. Demands for improved antenna size and resolution, as well as the space constraints of IUS, shuttle, and Titan IV, more than made up for any cost savings from using common bus architectures and electronic subsystems on the satellites. Each satellite was exceeding half a billion dollars in cost, so avoiding mishaps was critical. The NRO was lucky that money was not an object during most of the Reagan administration, until budget deficits began to force fiscal prudence at the Pentagon in the latter half of the 1980s. The vagaries of the black budget assured that few Americans understood that the NRO's annual budget now exceeded $5 billion. The lack of discipline eventually came back to hurt the agency, when NRO Director Jeff Harris was forced to resign in 1996 because of the NRO's lack of control over its own budget.

But during the 1980s, few noticed or cared about the runaway costs of collecting real-time intelligence from space.

While Chalet/Vortex was a revolution in its own right, offering far greater capabilities than its Rhyolite/Argon predecessor, Magnum was in a class all its own. John Pike, currently of GlobalSecurity.org and formerly with the Federation of American Scientists, estimated in a FAS study of Desert Storm that Magnum was twice the size of Vortex, with its focal point being 'not a single receiver, but rather a large array of feed horns.'[1] After the maiden Magnum mission on board the space shuttle in 1985, additional Magnums were launched in November 1989 and November 1990. The satellites came to some use during Operation Just Cause, to unseat Manuel Noriega of Panama, in December 1989, though Desert Storm represented the true fulfillment of Magnum capabilities.

The *Challenger* disaster of 1986 meant more than rescheduling satellite manifests for the Titan IV. In the first place, the giant rocket built at Martin-Marietta's (later Lockheed-Martin's) Waterton Canyon plant in southwest Denver, was far from reliable. A Navy cluster of White Cloud Follow-On ('Ranger') satellites blew up on a Titan IV in August 1993, and a Vortex/Mercury satellite was obliterated five years later in a similar Titan IV launch accident. One of the reasons the NRO placed heavy emphasis, and fairly significant expenditures, in the Evolved Expendable Launch Vehicle (EELV) program in the mid-1990s, was to reduce the costs encountered in Titan IV launches, while hopefully improving reliability in a new generation of rocket.

Other ground-based changes came about as a result of the *Challenger* disaster. In Colorado Springs, the Consolidated Space Operations Center, located at the re-christened Falcon Air Force Base (eventually to be re-named yet again for space pioneer Bernard Schriever), had a new mission replacing the former goal of managing military space shuttle missions. When the center opened in September 1985, it was responsible for controlling all major military satellite programs. That same month, the US Space Command was activated to oversee the Air Force, Army, and Navy Space Commands. Headquartered at Peterson Air Force Base in Colorado Springs, US Space Command would oversee the Falcon missions. With the demise of the shuttle, Falcon took on new duties in support of ballistic missile defense, and the simulation of space warfare.

It wasn't apparent by late 1986 that Falcon would have much to do in the SDIO support role. The X-ray laser had been shown to be unreliable and not powerful enough, when tested in underground H-bomb-powered tests at the Nevada Test Site. The initial optimistic results of the Dauphin tests in November 1980 were never replicated in a system that could be deployable, either in a battle station waiting in space for Armageddon, or in Edward Teller's favorite notion of an X-ray laser 'pop-up' satellite launched from a strategic submarine. Chemical lasers, while realizing some improvement in the mid-1980s through the application of adaptive mirror systems, still were far from deployable by 1986.

Two kinetic-kill systems, which would obliterate warheads simply by hitting them, were under consideration during the latter Reagan and Bush administrations: the space-based 'smart rock' program, later redefined by Edward Teller and Lowell Wood as Brilliant Pebbles; and the Exoatmospheric Re-entry vehicle Interceptor Subsystem, or ERIS. ERIS was a high-altitude version of the former HEDI (High Endo-atmospheric Defense Interceptor) rocket studied in the Carter years. When critics charged that boost-phase defense would require thousands of battle stations in space and hundreds of guidance nodes, Congress cut the Fiscal Year 1987 SDI budget from $5.4 billion to $3.5 billion.

This did not stop Caspar Weinberger. He announced in January 1987 that a 'Phase One' system was ready for deployment, apparently consisting of ERIS missiles plus some form of space-based 'smart-rock' system. Many elements of the system were so undefined, and the initial startup costs so great, that critics accused Weinberger of merely wishing to get an unstoppable program under way before Reagan left office, assuring that the ABM Treaty would be left in the dust as a result. The defense secretary had begun a classified project within the SDIO at the end of 1986 for a heavy-lift space vehicle and the capability to mass-produce 400 to 1,000 ERIS missiles, so his intention appeared genuine. But after Senator Sam Nunn denounced the administration's position on the ABM Treaty in mid-1987, and the Soviets later agreed to sign the Intermediate Nuclear Forces Treaty and leave Afghanistan, the impetus for near-term deployment of missile-defense elements no longer existed. In fact, FitzGerald points out that many Space Command officials made comments in early 1988 that could be interpreted as being opposed to weapons in space, a far cry from their views in the following decade.[2]

One weapon system that did catch Space Command's eye, however, was a moving-target indicator and assault program, not considered part of SDI in the 1980s, but later considered integral to overall theater defense. Joint Surveillance Target Attack Reconnaissance System, or Joint-STARS, was an Army/Air Force program that grew out of a deep-strike project within the Air Force called Pave Mover. The idea was to use an E8C aircraft with a multi-mode phased array radar to fly in a standoff position from a line of battle, and identify moving targets for later missile or smart-bomb attack. Space Command got to observe the Joint-STARS system second-hand as it prepared communication systems for the deep-strike aircraft, and the Joint-STARS performance during the Gulf War was impressive enough to make Space Command cognizant of the role radar and moving-target indication would play for both global conflict management, and theater missile defense.

While the elder George Bush often is remembered as a partial friend to arms control because of his role in concluding the START II Treaty, the first six months of his administration were characterized by such inaction on rationalizing weapons systems that even Reagan criticized some of his positions as too hardline. Both John Tower, Bush's first choice for defense secretary, and his later chosen secretary Dick Cheney, recognized the unpopularity of SDI, but Bush insisted on keeping defensive weapons well-funded, even if a Phase One deployment no longer was talked about. In April 1989, Cheney funded a new architectural study for 4,600 Brilliant Pebbles satellites in orbit, accompanied by 1,000–2,000 ground-based interceptors.

The collapse of the Berlin Wall and the liberation of eastern European states at the end of 1989 did little to change the Bush view, which immediately shifted to one of using Brilliant Pebbles against Iraq and independent terrorist groups (the anti-Iraq rhetoric preceded Iraq's August 1990 invasion of Kuwait, primarily because of growing concern over Saddam Hussein's use of Scuds in the Persian Gulf shipping battles). This view was codified in early 1991 in the Global Protection Against Limited Strikes, or GPALS plan, which called for 1,000 Brilliant Pebbles in space and 500–600 ground-based interceptors, at an anticipated cost of $40 billion. It is certainly true that, with the Soviet Union in discussions to eliminate portions of its missile arsenal, the main rationale for fielding missile-defense weapons was to meet a much smaller threat from China and emerging states with intermediate-range missiles. This would make a missile-defense system easier to build, since the number of missiles anticipated in an assault could be reduced by several factors, if not orders of magnitude. But it is also true that the old 1967 message of ballistic missile-defense serving offensive strategies more than genuine defensive ones, originally promulgated in a bipolar superpower era, carried even more weight when a single superpower held an untrumpable advantage over any other nation on the planet. This was recognized explicitly by Cheney and many others in the Defense Department, throughout the transition period from SDI to GPALS: 'From the beginning it had been clear to many experts that Star Wars technologies were much better suited to the offense than to the defense, and among Star Wars enthusiasts there were a number who had always thought that the goal of the program should be to establish U.S. control over space,' FitzGerald wrote, in *Way Out There in the Blue*.

Meanwhile, Bush was fully cognizant of the opportunity to better coordinate the work of the NSA, the NRO, and Space Command. He hired Duane Andrews to head up a new Defense Department post on Command, Control, Communications, and Intelligence, to oversee interagency disputes. He also decentralized some tasks from the CIA and the NRO, creating a Central Imagery Office in the Pentagon to handle image intelligence. As part of the effort to get NRO information to the field in a more timely fashion, Bush decided to declassify the NRO's existence, mission, and portions of its history in late 1992. NRO Director Martin Faga took the order seriously, and the NRO developed a reputation during the 1990s of being even more forthcoming with press and academia on its mission and plans than the NSA.

Because of loosened restrictions on the distribution of intelligence during the Reagan and Bush years, word began to spread around the Pentagon on the improved capabilities demonstrated by the newer highly-classified imaging and signals satellites, as well as by the more open DSP early-warning system. Signals intelligence from space had played a critical role in the reflagging battles of the Persian Gulf in 1987, and DSP had tracked tactical missile developments in Israel, India, and South Africa at the end of the decade. Between Saddam Hussein's invasion of Kuwait in August 1990 and the subsequent January 1991 US attack on Iraq, the Joint Chiefs of Staff ruled that DSP data could be sent directly to tactical commanders, rather than being shuttled through third parties.

This had little practical effect in the Gulf War, in using DSP to enhance the Patriot missile response to Scud missile attacks on Israel. While several officers in the Israeli Defense Forces felt that the Patriot was an oversold missile system to begin with, Richelson showed in his DSP study that the Tactical Event Reporting System developed for relaying DSP information to the Gulf was far too cumbersome. Information was relayed to Buckley Field in Colorado, then sent to a Naval Security Group base at Skaggs Island near Vallejo, California, from there to a DSCS-2 satellite, and finally to a specialized tactical terminal in Israel. To no one's great surprise, the information came too late to be of value in many Scud attacks.

The future of DSP was tied up in how tightly it was to be integrated with SDI weapons. The initial planned Advanced Warning System, meant to replace DSP, was killed after Reagan's March 1983 speech, only to resurface within the SDIO as the Boost Surveillance and Tracking System in 1985. But in 1990, Duane Andrews and new NRO Director Martin Faga shifted Boost Surveillance back to the Air Force from the SDIO. The missile-defense developers decided that the missile-launch intelligence provided by DSP was worthy as a separate system, and that missile tracking for a defensive system should be done in a separate Brilliant Pebbles network. The resulting portion outside Brilliant Pebbles was the system that was re-named Follow-On Early Warning System, or FEWS, which Space Command head Charles Horner later was accused of promoting past the point where its capabilities made sense. Regardless of the flap over DSP's many planned successors, however, it is important to realize that military planners understood the value of the system for large-scale warfare prior to the 1991 attack on Iraq – they simply did not have the elements in place to exploit the system fully. The same would be true for GPS – by the time of the Afghan war of 2001, GPS would be directing individual gravity bombs. But ten years earlier, GPS was used primarily for guiding ships and planes. To be fair, GPS receivers used by ground troops were absolutely essential in executing the end run around the western desert of Kuwait which Gen. Norman Schwarzkopf made the centerpiece of his 1991 land assault on Iraq. But GPS as an enabler for precision bombing was still several years away from common use.

It is often suggested that, although only a third of the bombs used in the early air assaults on Iraq in January 1991 were precision weapons, they scored more than two-thirds of the successful hits in Kuwait and Iraq. But it is important to clarify what 'precision' meant in Desert Storm. The only precision bombs present in the war were the laser-guided bombs carried on several US bombers and fighters, and individual cruise missiles with their Terrain Contour Matching System, in which a targeting system had to rely on stored map images. Regular use of space was far from normal in the Gulf War, where overwhelming superiority in air, naval, and ground forces carried the day.

Nevertheless, the vision of using space as part of a forward-based, offensive strategy was clear long before Desert Storm and its Desert Shield buildup. Pike, in his FAS study of Desert Storm, correctly suggested that it was impossible to understand military space in the 1990s without grasping the doctrinal intent of AirLand Battle 2000 scenarios, the missions of the Joint-STARS air war, or the overall concepts of Deep Strike warfare. AirLand Battle was developed in the waning years of the Cold War in order to devise non-nuclear ways of defeating the Soviets in the long-feared event of a 'Fulda Gap' ground assault on Western Europe. It relied on not addressing an assault head-on, but going after the enemy's rear flanks through 'deep strikes.' AirLand Battle was an ideal strategy to use in a unipolar world where the US sought to dominate all theaters, but it required more immediate intelligence than local tactical commanders were receiving.

Since the early 1980s, all military service commanders had realized that the key to using strategic space assets was to expand and implement the tactical intelligence program known as TENCAP, or Tactical Exploitation of National Capabilities. Rudimentary aspects of TENCAP, in which ground forces could use satellite terminals with delayed and incomplete intelligence information, had been in place during the invasion of Grenada and the Marine deployment to Lebanon during Reagan's first term. By the time of the Panama invasion, and of the early preparations for Desert Shield, troop units had access to special TENCAP terminals called Constant Source, and FIST (Fleet Imagery Support Terminal). Constant Source, the platform in which NSA and the Defense Intelligence Agency pioneered their Binocular intelligence-distribution system, was a direct precursor to the powerful worldwide system later known as Global Broadcast System. Just as GBS used the Navy's UHF Follow-On satellite as a one-way broadband intelligence distribution network, Constant Source used a channel on the Navy FLTSATCOM UHF system to provide a narrowband, partial equivalent of the capabilities that would later be present on GBS.

The only problem in the buildup to Desert Storm was the delay, as much bureaucratic as technological, in providing intelligence to forces on the ground and in the air. There certainly was no shortage of available space assets. During the period between the August 1990 Kuwait invasion and the February 1991 withdrawal, there were three KH-11 imaging satellites in orbit; one Lacrosse radar satellite; at least one Magnum, plus 15–20 secondary signals intelligence satellites such as Vortex, White Cloud, and Ferret; two Defense Meteorological Satellite Program satellites; two DSCS-3 communication satellites; 15–16 GPS satellites; and two FLTSATCOM Navy communication satellites.

The KH-11 satellites represented a significant improvement over earlier imaging satellites, because their starlight scopes allowed them to take pictures 24 hours a day. But cloud cover still was a problem, particularly in the first week of the air assault in Desert Storm, when weather over Iraq was the worst seen in several months. Consequently, the launch of the first Lacrosse radar satellite in December 1988 provided military commanders with an all-weather resource they did not have previously. Lacrosse, based on a Project Indigo design of the late 1970s approved by then-CIA Director George Bush, was approved as a production satellite in 1983. Its final design had a solar array 50 meters wide to provide power of tens of kilowatts. It could provide radar-frequency image resolution of less than one meter – still not as good as the best photographic imaging satellites, but good for an initial space-radar capability. In the period immediately following the initial Iraqi invasion of Kuwait, the US Central Command had to rely on Lacrosse as much or more than the KH-11, to keep track of the new 'mobile' Scud missile systems on board flatbed trucks.

Before the air assault on Iraq began on January 16, 1991, the Air Force established a special classified team called Checkmate to develop a unified database of bomb targets. The bombing plan, Instant Thunder, was based on satellite intelligence, though at that time, NRO information was never sent directly to Central Command, but had to be filtered through multiple Washington agencies. In a study of overall Air Force and Navy operations, military analyst Norman Friedman said that the Air Force's Air Tasking Order system required a dedicated Airborne Command and Control Center on C-130 planes. This made it difficult for Navy planes, as well as British and Israeli forces, to participate in anything more than a tangential sense, in the Instant Thunder planning.[3]

The initial attack on Iraqi air defense nevertheless fulfilled its mission, relying on Air Force/NSA Rivet Joint intelligence planes and EC-130H Compass Call jamming planes as key elements of foiling Iraqi response to attack. The initial strikes in Desert Storm were specialized attacks on high-frequency Iraqi radars carried out by helicopters armed with laser-guided missiles. These were followed by HARM missile and Tomahawk cruise-missile assaults that took out the primary air-defense Tall King radars, and F-117 attacks that took out Iraq's unfortified, centralized air-defense control centers. Friedman says that Iraq's reliance on a centralized and unprotected air-defense system doomed the Iraqi military within the first few hours of the air war. However, he also points out that air intelligence was spotty, and that lack of immediate access to space intelligence made all the difference in the world. 'The coalition lacked organic reconnaissance,' Friedman wrote. 'It could not easily target aircraft on a timely basis.'

While these aspects became less important at the end of February, when the overwhelming success of the land assaults swept aside other issues, those closest to the battles never forgot the limitations in Desert Storm to implementing precision warfare. It is interesting to note that those military officers most vociferous early in the Clinton administration for using space to achieve planetary dominance, were those making the strongest pitches for air power in the post-Iraq months of the Bush administration. Gen. Merrill McPeak, the Air Force Chief of Staff who forcefully insisted on Space Command's domination of space in April 1993, was lobbying then-Joint Chiefs of Staff Chairman Colin Powell in mid-1992 to use the new tools of air power to assault Serb positions in Croatia and Bosnia. Similarly, Gen. Charles Horner, head of the Space Command in the early 1990s, headed up the air campaign in Desert Storm, and began advocating using space as a battlefield virtually as soon as the Iraq campaign was concluded.

The moderating factor, both before and after the 1992 campaign, was the reticence of the civilian leadership on either Republican or Democrat sides to strike so brash a position so soon after the Soviet Union's demise. Bush, despite his late appreciation of the depth of change in Russia, went out of his way to avoid gloating over the demise of the eastern European socialist states at the end of 1989, or the later end of the Soviet Union in December 1991. He sought to treat Gorbachev fairly, and to transfer support to Boris Yeltsin when the latter politician proved the more important horse to back during the attempted hardline Soviet coup in August 1991. His continued efforts to reduce nuclear arsenals in conjunction with the new Russian republic, even after he had lost the 1992 election with Clinton, shows that George Bush had internalized the opportunity to truly reduce the level of alert between the superpowers, as a result of the profound changes in Russia.

Certainly, the desire to play according to coalition rules, and to avoid upsetting the real opportunity to end the Cold War, played into the Bush decision to tell Schwarzkopf and Powell not to pursue Saddam Hussein into Baghdad at the end of the Gulf War. It also made Bush and his lame-duck Secretary of State, Lawrence Eagleburger, reticent to take too hard a line on Serbia.

There is no indication that Bush would have made any real efforts to reduce the global network of nuclear-weapon support bases, and UKUSA intelligence bases, had he been re-elected in 1992. But he presented Clinton with a golden opportunity, which the incoming president clearly threw away.

In assessing the differences between Clinton and Bush, however, it is important to understand the overwhelming popularity of the unilateralist model in Washington following the Soviet Union's demise. Multilateralism was a useful fig leaf to borrow when the US did not wish to overplay its triumphalist card, but there was no true constituency outside the minuscule peace community for realizing a peace dividend by cutting back on strategic weapons or intelligence networks. In the final analysis, both major US parties perceived global management of all nations by the surviving superpower as right and proper, because the US was seen by all in the Washington power elite as the only nation qualified to own the rulebooks.

Clinton, as a dedicated member of the conservative Democratic Leadership Council, wishing to masquerade as a liberal, pretended to be interested in continued good relations with the Russians and possible reduced defense budgets, but had too little interest in foreign policy to take the initiative on redefining national security. Besides, the power of what Michael Klare calls 'permanent pre-eminence' held sway over both Republicans and Democrats in Washington. Perhaps only arch-conservatives wanted to gloat over the US 'winning the Cold War.' But even the centrists of the Democratic Party and the diminishing Republican international wing saw little value in moving to true multilateralism, or taking any action that would reduce US dominance of the planet.

Clinton was not given the opportunity to remain aloof on foreign policy issues for long, as the twin crises of Bosnia and Somalia forced him to pay attention to matters he wished would remain peripheral to his agenda. The embarrassments caused by the assault on Army Rangers in Somalia, and the failure to move to air strikes on Serb forces in Srebrenica, often are cited by conservatives as proof positive that multilateralism won't work. The reticence to engage anywhere was a factor that prevented both the US and European partners from rescuing Tutsis from the Hutu massacre in Rwanda in April 1994. There were indeed aspects of both Somalia and Bosnia that soured the administration from participating in multilateralism as traditionally defined, though the circumstances were more nuanced than conservatives assume.

In an intriguing study of national security operations during Clinton's two terms in office, *War in a Time of Peace*, author David Halberstam puts partial blame on Colin Powell for the

Somalia debacle. Halberstam points out that Powell, during the waning months of the Bush administration, betrayed his own doctrine of avoiding peripheral troop commitments, in virtually volunteering two divisions for humanitarian missions in the dissolving state of Somalia. Halberstam also finds fault with the controversial UN Secretary General Boutros Boutros-Ghali, for leading the conversion of a humanitarian troop mission into a hunt for Somali clan leader Mohammed Farah Aidid. The resulting 'Black Hawk Down' fiasco led to the death of 18 US troops, and the television images of alleged Good Samaritans being dragged through the streets. The disaster was one factor leading to the early departure of Defense Secretary Les Aspin.[4]

Meanwhile, Secretary of State Warren Christopher had been chastened during a tour of Europe in May 1993, in which the administration sought 'consultation' on the viability of air strikes against Serb positions in the Srebrenica area. Certainly, Clinton cabinet members were uniformly upset about the brash attitudes of forces under Serb General Radko Mladic, since NRO images showed that the Serbs were making no efforts to hide their large cannons, assuming rightly that NATO would not agree on a 'lift and strike' air assault. After being rebuffed by NATO allies during his visit, Christopher came back to Washington finding full support in the Clinton cabinet for his view that the era of 'consultation' was dead. From now on, allies should be told what the US planned to do, and they should simply be notified that they could join or not join in a mission, but that the mission would be decided solely by US planners.

This view formed the basis for US air strikes on Bosnia in August 1995, as well as the Kosovo war of 1999. Because Madeleine Albright always had a more unilateralist stance than Christopher or National Security Advisor Anthony Lake, her move to the State Department position in the second Clinton administration only accelerated the move to pure unilateralism. But even prior to that time, the message of the US being the sole decider of its global interests had permeated into the intelligence and military-space community.

At the 1993 National Space Symposium, Gen. Merrill McPeak's keynote speech on dominating the planet had seemed somewhat over the top. But in the two succeeding years, Maj. Gen. Robert Parker, the director of operations at Air Force Space Command, boasted that the Space Warfare Center's hosting of the Talon missions represented the fruition of an 'In your face from outer space' goal. Meanwhile, NRO Director Jeff Harris boasted in a 1995 Space Symposium speech of moving 'terabyte miles per second' of data from spy satellites to soldiers in the field.

As word of the new overt doctrines reached arms controllers in Washington, several centrist groups sought private meetings with White House advisors about the strange and boastful messages emanating from Space Command. They were told that this was a case of the Pentagon going a little overboard in its brashness, and that the mission of using the NRO and Space Command for planetary management was not explicitly supported by the White House. While there may not be direct evidence for Clinton asking the Space Command to launch its 'full-spectrum dominance' campaign, there is enough circumstantial evidence to suggest that Space Command rhetoric represented the mainstream White House view. Defense Secretary William Perry encouraged the US Space Command's development of the *Vision for 2020* document, based on Joint Chiefs Chairman John Shalikashvili's approval of the multi-service *Joint Vision 2010* program. While Shalikashvili is not typically known as a unilateralist, the *JV2010* program explicitly called for 'dominant maneuver, precision engagement, full-dimensional protection, and focused logistics' to be able to dominate air, sea, land, and space.

Even prior to completion of the *Vision for 2020* document in 1996,[5] the Space Warfare Center at Schriever Air Force Base was able to demonstrate the broadening of the TENCAP program, through hosting the Talon missions in the early 1990s. A suite of Talon projects focusing on the distribution of intelligence to field commanders, had been split among Peterson, Schriever, and other bases, until the Space Warfare Center opened at Schriever in 1993. From then on, programs such as Talon Vision, Talon Warrior, Talon Knight, Talon Outlook, Talon Shooter, and Talon Ready were run out of the center. In July 1995, species-specific TENCAP programs in the Talon series were combined in a live test involving the transfer of NRO and NSA information to fighter jets, battleships, and individual special-operations soldiers in the field. The successful results of Project Strike led to the implementation of a regular broadband communication architecture, the Global Broadcast System, and a pattern of establishing virtual 'space bases' in every theater of war. The post-Talon model was applied in Kosovo and Colombia before coming full flower in the October 2001 assault on Afghanistan.

In the meantime, however, the NRO faced some uncommon scrutiny from Congress. In 1993, the agency was secretly slammed for continuing to let contracts for a space-based Wide-Area Surveillance System (predecessor to the Space-Based Radar), after Congress called for funding to end. In the summer of 1994, hearings were held on the $350 million headquarters the NRO was building in Chantilly, Virginia, though agency officials could show members of key committees that they had voted for those same expenditures in earlier sessions. The NRO's problems hit true crisis point in late 1995, however, when the agency admitted to not being able to account for $1 billion of its $6 billion annual budget. The chief financial officer of the NRO was replaced. When the unaudited amounts hit $2.5 billion in February 1996, however, Director of Central Intelligence John Deutch removed both NRO Director Harris, and Deputy Director Jimmie Hill. It took incoming director Keith Hall several months to put the agency's affairs in order, but Hall arrived with a natural proclivity for seeing total space dominance as right and proper. He reiterated a famous line in several public speeches that was later borrowed by his successor Peter Teets: 'In regard to space dominance, we have it, we like it, and we're going to keep it.'

The final push to unilateralism took place between the publication of *Vision for 2020* in 1996 and the assault on Kosovo in 1999. Clinton was slightly distracted, of course, by the sex scandal that led to his impeachment hearings. But Al Gore and Madeleine Albright, both strong supporters of unilateralism, saw to it that what the Space Command was arguing in theory, was supported by US actions on the ground. In the meantime, the ballistic missile defense element of space dominance, in the background since Clinton's arrival in Washington, was propelled to the foreground by the 1994 Republican Contract with America, and the 1998 Rumsfeld Commission on the ballistic missile threat.

7
BMDO, '3+3,' and the New Missile Threat

Because ballistic missile defense was not considered a central element of the Clinton administration vision, hawkish critics like Rep. Curt Weldon often assume that the transition from SDIO to Clinton's rechristened Ballistic Missile Defense Organization meant that missile defense had entered its lean, deep-freeze years. Oddly enough, though, BMDO funding levels always kept pace with SDIO in the range of $2–$5 billion per year, though the steep escalation anticipated for a near-term deployment never showed up during Clinton's eight years in office.

This was not a case of simple foot-dragging. BMDO and the Defense Advanced Research Projects Agency wisely insisted on fielding something that worked, and held the ground-based program to sensible standards of viability. Under a normal testing regime, ERIS and THAAD (Theater High Altitude Area Defense) projects simply were not up to snuff, and continued tests did not improve the outlook for a near-term deployment schedule.

Because so little attention was paid to service-specific theater missile-defense (TMD) programs, many Republican analysts tried to paint the Clinton years, particularly the first term, as a time when nothing was happening. While few experiments made headlines, there was plenty going on. The US Army's Space and Strategic Defense Command, for example, expanded a program to test bogus Scud missiles in flights over Canyonlands National Park in Utah, El Malpais National Monument in New Mexico, and the Shalomar/Fort Walton Beach regions on the Florida panhandle. Although nationwide environmental hearings were held on the tests in 1994, little attention was paid to the program at first, because it was seen as a simple tactical upgrade of the Patriot missile to its PAC-3 version. It became clear, however, that such upgrades would directly serve TMD programs for allies such as South Korea and Taiwan. (Israel insisted on its own joint TMD program, using the Arrow missile, due to its deep skepticism on Patriot capabilities.)

The program faced significant citizen opposition in Utah and New Mexico, where major roads would have to be closed when Scuds were launched from Fort Wingate, NM and Green River, Utah to landing sites at White Sands Missile Range. But members of the policy elite were silenced through two important factors: First, the demand for increased tests was taking place simultaneously with the 1994 North Korea crisis, where Clinton came close to considering a strike at North Korean nuclear facilities in response to new efforts by Kim Il Sung's regime to go nuclear. Second, the Clinton administration had already made known its desire to make 'minor' modifications to the ABM Treaty, in order to use Patriot TMD tests as a means of fine-tuning the THAAD development program. As an indication of how this argument played with the centrist policy wonks, Sidney Graybeal and Michael Krepon argued in the April 1994 *Bulletin of the Atomic Scientists* that TMD tests should be supported by ABM advocates as an acceptable 'fix' that could keep the ABM Treaty alive. In retrospect, one could make the more convincing case that the Army TMD tests were the first effort to put the foot in the door that eventually led to George Bush's scrapping of the ABM Treaty in 2002.

Hawaii also played host to continued TMD tests throughout the so-called lean years. The Strategic Target System (STARS) was conceived at Sandia National Labs as a general-purpose rocket, meant to simulate ICBM characteristics, which could be launched from Barking Sands on Kauai, Hawaii for interception over Kwajalein. The first rocket launch in February 1993 was met by widespread protest and civil disobedience. By the time a STARS rocket was used in August 1996 as part of the BMDO Midcourse Space Experiment, however, protests had dwindled. By that time, use of Kauai and the nearby private island of Ni'ihau by the Navy and BMDO had become so commonplace, anti-BMD activists were somewhat overwhelmed. The Army stirred up a new degree of concern by proposing the Kodiak Launch Facility on Kodiak Island in Alaska as another STARS site, but the pro-military organizations in Alaska were touting joint commercial and military purposes for Kodiak with such fervor that the skeptical voices were all but drowned out.

The pro-BMD organizations in Washington consistently argued that these tactical programs for radar expansion and launch site preparation were nothing more than bare-minimum R&D, and that the lack of a deployable weapon system proved how much the Clinton administration was obstructing BMD. The problem with this argument is that there was nothing functional to deploy (a factor that never stopped Bush's Missile Defense Agency a decade later, however). The expansion of these low-profile BMDO operations also served as a foot in the door for making missile defense seem normal.

In Hawaii, an unmanned radar site on Ni'ihau served to grease the skids for having the Robinson family, which owned the island, consider additional radar facilities and unmanned sensors and jammers. The Navy and DARPA sponsored a program called Mountain Top 2, tying together high-altitude radars on Makaha Ridge in Kauai with White Sands Missile Range radars, to test the capability of detecting stealth aircraft and depressed-trajectory cruise missiles. The Navy also pushed both NASA and the intelligence community to expand test flights of unpiloted aerial vehicles (UAVs) in the Pacific Missile Test Range, to hone the use of UAVs in Kosovo and elsewhere.[1]

Similarly, the existing BMEWS radars at Clear, Alaska; Flyingdales, England; and Thule, Greenland were upgraded in the mid-1990s with larger flat-faced phased-array radars based on the PAVE PAWS design. The upgrade was partially funded by BMDO, which wanted better boost-phase detection of missiles, and also wanted the local citizens accustomed to the idea of base expansion, when new X-band radar systems would be rolled out at all three sites as an integral part of BMD.

Two other radar programs received little attention during their rollout in mid-decade, despite their critical role in missile defense. The Massachusetts Institute of Technology's Lincoln Labs, along with Mitre Corp., designed a dish version of a radar called Cobra Gemini, meant to be installed on Navy T-AGOS ships. The Cobra Gemini project, also known as Steel Trap, was promoted by the new Central MASINT (Measurement and Signatures Intelligence) Office, or CMO, which wanted a dual-frequency radar covering both the X-band and S-band, capable of spotting short-range missiles from land or sea. Cobra Gemini was meant to augment the older Cobra Judy program, a shipboard radar that searched for intercontinental missiles. While BMDO and CMO could claim that the Gemini adjunct was a purely defensive project, its use in TMD scenarios for theater battles, such as naval skirmishes in the Taiwan Straits or the seas off Korea, suggest that the Defense Department had long considered Cobra Gemini's role in first-strike warfare. One ship, the *Invincible*, was turned over to Space Command in 2000 for active duty in the Cobra Gemini program.

A similar land-based program sponsored by Space Command served as a semi-covert means of testing out high-power X-band radars for space surveillance. The Have Stare radar system was developed at Vandenberg Air Force Base in the mid-1990s, then transferred to Vardo, Norway in 1999 under the cover name of Globus II, where it is run by the Norwegian Military Intelligence Agency. A detailed analysis of the Vardo project in the March/April 2000 *Bulletin of the Atomic Scientists* concluded that the intense secrecy for this multi-purpose BMD and space sur-veillance program may be due to its proximity to the Russian border. Earlier programs at Vardo were used in tracking SLBMs off the Kola Peninsula, and the location of the Have Stare radar would seem to suggest that the BMDO, at least in the late 1990s, still considered Russia a possible source of hostile missile attack, something the Russian government would be none too keen to learn.[2]

In the optical domain, the Air Force's Starfire Optical Range, which opened in 1995 at a location near Kirtland Air Force Base, New Mexico, provides better opportunities to image objects in low-earth orbit than does the Ground-Based Electro-Optical Deep Space Surveillance telescope in nearby Socorro, NM. By using active lasers to illuminate objects, Starfire can provide images in much greater detail than passive sensors. Starfire was used in February 2003 to provide the most detailed images of the *Columbia* shuttle prior to its catastrophic breakup.

The Clinton era, therefore, was a time when many significant systems related to missile defense and space battle management were fielded. What relevance can be assigned, then, to the 1998 Commission to Assess the Ballistic Missile Threat to the United States, chaired by none other than Donald Rumsfeld? Bradley Graham of the *Washington Post*, in his book on Clinton-era BMD programs, *Hit to Kill*, concludes with some justification that

Rumsfeld was able to achieve near-perfect consensus in his panel because of the degree of exasperation commission members experienced in dealing with CIA analysts, who were unwilling to look at possible crash programs in developing-nation missile development that could accelerate a missile threat from a smaller state.[3] It is certainly true that the North Korean timeline for developing the Taepodong II three-stage intermediate missile made the CIA's National Intelligence Estimate of 1995 look downright silly. The CIA claimed at the time that any multi-stage intermediate missile program from a developing state would not bear fruit for more than five years. Rumsfeld had a point in blasting the CIA for failing to apprehend that a nation could develop a multi-stage rocket in a faster timetable than the five years the agency predicted – and the August 1998 test of a Taepodong II bore out that criticism.

Rumsfeld, however, was well-known for adopting a worst-case analysis that would minimize the US threat to others while treating every potential threat to the US as a real one. His role in a later commission on military space, which released its report just prior to Bush's inauguration, would demonstrate this tendency, occasionally to ridiculous extremes. And independent groups like the Federation of American Scientists were quick to poke holes in the North Korean 'threat,' showing the rudimentary state of launch facilities in the near-starving nation.

Clinton, in order to counter pro-deployment pressure from the Heritage Foundation and the Bob Dole/Newt Gingrich 'Defend America' bill, called for a '3+3' program, in which three years of missile-defense development would be followed, if it was warranted given international conditions, by three years of deployment, allowing a national missile defense system to be put in place as early as 2003. Privately, BMDO officials realized that even the most mature of the ground-based systems, the Patriot PAC-3 and THAAD programs, could not meet such a rushed schedule.

While '3+3' would no doubt require an ABM Treaty breakout at some future date, many Republicans were ready to renounce the treaty by the time the Rumsfeld Commission released its report in the summer of 1998. What neither the Clinton administration nor its critics stopped to ask, however, was what kind of threat a small nation, even one committed to a crash course in missile development, might truly pose to a unilateral superpower with multiple layers of precision weapons. Of course, the US was right to push for an end to missile-technology-sharing programs through the official multilateral body, Missile Technology Control Regime. Of course, the nation had to remain vigilant regarding the capabilities of the Taepodong II, the Indian Agni and Prithvi missiles, the Pakistani Ghaur missiles, and several other developing-nation derivatives of the popular Scud. But the decidedly different reactions to the 1998 nuclearization of India and Pakistan, as compared to the potential threat of longer-range Taepodong II missiles, showed that the 1998 debate was not about which developing nations gained access to weapons of mass destruction and the means to deliver them. The real debate was about having an overwhelming, trump-card response to those nations which would dare challenge US global reach in a direct way. Certainly, the US State Department was worried about nuclear weapons in the hands of India and Pakistan, particularly as the squabbling over Kashmir grew worse at decade's end. But the furor over North Korea in late 1998, which remained a belligerent but rather pathetic nation in terms of its projection capability, was far greater than what was warranted. New entrants to the nuclear club, even in unstable regions like South Asia, were begrudgingly accepted if the nations' leaderships accepted the international pecking order. The few 'rogue states' that questioned such a pecking order became the new threats, and their missile capabilities were inflated to a greater extent than was warranted, to help sell BMD.

On a practical basis, the technical capabilities of NRO satellites were foiled by a gross inability of human analysts to interpret what they were seeing. The failure to anticipate India's nuclear-bomb test of 1998, for example, led Clinton to appoint Ret. Adm. David Jeremiah, the author of an internal NRO study called the 'Jeremiah Report', to look at what went wrong. Spotting several failures of individual human analysts who had access to information on the India test site in a timely manner, Jeremiah concluded that spy satellite technology had vastly outstripped the capability of humans to process the information.

Regardless of who was to blame for not tracking missile development and nuclear proliferation, even the most skeptical of White House and Pentagon analysts could ascertain which way the political winds were blowing. An interagency meeting on December 11, 1998, locked in what the Pentagon would announce the following month: the White House would seek increases in missile-defense funding, and would broach with Russia the sensitive topic of modifying the ABM Treaty. A solid decision on deployment, however, would not come until 2000.

The BMDO program in Clinton's first term had been solidly oriented to theater programs, which meant Patriot upgrades and THAAD work for the Army, and two more ethereal programs for the Navy. For shorter-range defense, the Navy was developing a program that would combine existing Aegis missile cruisers, complete with the SPY-1 radar to track short-range missiles, with an upgraded defensive missile. The longer-range program, a theater-wide project for fending off intermediate-range missiles, never took solid shape before the Bush administration canceled many Navy TMD programs in 2001.

What changed with the meeting at the end of 1998 was that greater emphasis was placed upon National Missile Defense, for which the BMDO already had defined six concrete elements by mid-decade. In space, the NMD program would use existing DSP satellites, but augment them with a new two-tier system, Space-Based Infrared System, or SBIRS. SBIRS-High would entail more advanced infrared satellites in geostationary orbit, along with two or more Heritage-like infrared sensors on board secret signals intelligence satellites in elliptical orbit. SBIRS-Low, slated to come later to augment the discrimination of sensors to weed out warhead decoys, would consist of 24 satellites in low-earth orbit, utilizing some of the sensing technology developed for Brilliant Eyes. Not only was the technology for SBIRS-Low less developed than that for SBIRS-High, but Clinton administration officials were rightly worried that Russia and China would see the lower-orbit system as the greater potential threat to a feasible ABM Treaty.

A second element of NMD was a network of new UHF radars around the world, meant to track the incoming warheads identified by SBIRS and DSP. A higher profile in radar deployment was assumed by the third element, large X-band radars meant to replace the phased-array early-warning radars in Alaska, Fylingdales, and Thule. An interceptor booster rocket with exoatmospheric kill vehicle, using design concepts from ERIS and

THAAD, was the fourth component. The fifth was the kill vehicle itself, incorporating a multi-bandwidth optical and infrared sensor. Finally, BMDO was designing a Battle Management Command/Control/Communications network, complete with ground-based control centers, to manage the kill vehicle.

None of these programs addressed the longer-term laser programs, either the Airborne Laser or Space-Based Laser. Steady incremental progress had been made in both systems since the mid-1980s, but neither system was close to being ready for even prototype testing by late 1998. It is interesting to note that five years later, many projects of the Space-Based Laser program office, expanded with much fanfare in the early days of the Bush administration, were canceled or postponed when the re-christened Missile Defense Agency realized how far from fruition directed-energy weapons in space really were. This cutback came despite the fact that the Bush administration was more than willing in 2003 to field ground-based missile-defense weapons without adequate testing.

The Airborne Laser program grew out of an experiment with roots in the early 1980s, when the Airborne Laser Lab was touted in the aftermath of Reagan's 1983 speech. An official program office for the airborne program was set up at Kirtland Air Force Base in New Mexico in 1992. For the first three years, the program was kept in dormant status while contractors completed an upgrade of the Chemical Oxygen Iodine Laser, or COIL, combining the original laser with adaptive, deformable mirrors that could compensate for turbulence in the atmosphere. Beginning in 1995, the office was upgraded to operational status with the participation of Boeing, TRW, and Lockheed-Martin. The plans at that time were to show that a modified 747 could shoot down a warhead in a realistic test regime by the end of fiscal 2003. In March 2001, subcontractor Raytheon Electronic Systems achieved 'first light' of the solid-state tracking laser that would track a target for the COIL laser.

The Space-Based Laser program by the late 1990s had given up on X-ray weapons requiring a nuclear explosion for a power source. Instead, 'Team SBL,' the troika of Lockheed-Martin, TRW, and Boeing, was designing a space-based system using the hydrogen-fluoride Alpha laser, an 8-megawatt laser that would require a fire-control computer system for each battle station in space. One such SBL platform would weigh as much as 77,000 pounds, or almost three times as heavy as the Hubble Space Telescope. In a study on Space-Based Lasers for DARPA, William Possel of the Air Force's SBL Office identified one obvious problem for such a large system: based on current capabilities of the Titan IV and possible follow-ons, at least two separate launches would be required for each SBL battle station, with assembly required in space. Early recognition of this problem spurred the BMDO into defining a 'small,' $3 billion Integrated Flight Experiment, which could be launched by an Evolved Expendable Launch Vehicle in 2012. Enthusiasm for this initial program, along with an appropriate dollop of pork-barrel politics, was responsible for promotion of a Space-Based Laser program at the Stennis Space Center in Mississippi. A viable network of satellites capable of performing boost-phase defense would require at least twelve battle stations in orbit, necessitating abrogation of both the ABM Treaty and Outer Space Treaty. As will be shown later, the original program for demonstration systems by 2012 was too aggressive, even for the gung-ho Bush team that followed Clinton.

While the ABL is perceived as primarily a theater defense weapon, SBL can have a role in both national missile defense and in what is known as 'counterspace' operations, which include anti-satellite missions. Even those within the military are worried about the implications of the latter duty, however. Col. Kenneth Barker of Wright-Patterson AFB's simulation program warned in the defense survey, *The Technological Arsenal*, that '[counterspace] operations are belligerent by nature, however, and undermine the notion that space is a sanctuary for peaceful purposes.' While Barker said that the implications of such operations made them 'politically untenable for now,' Space Command had issued the *Vision for 2020* and *Long-Range Plan* documents, which advocated positions that were indeed belligerent by nature.[4]

An alternative to actual lasers based in space is to use ground-based lasers, like the COIL in ABL, positioned in regions with very good weather, to aim at prepositioned mirrors in space for effective weapons that can take out warheads in flight. New Mexico peace groups who claim that the forementioned Starfire Optical Range is primarily a missile-defense program, are absolutely correct: Starfire's ability to illuminate a deteriorating shuttle on February 1, 2003 indicates that it could serve as the test range for a network of ground-based lasers aiming at a network as sparse as only four mirrors in geosynchronous orbit. Possel estimated the cost of a moderate ground-based system to be $61 billion, including $20.6 billion for five ground-based sites, and $40 billion for a network of mirrors in space, including the launch costs.

Directed-energy weapons in missile-defense applications got little publicity in the late 1990s, though, as the near-term debates centered on ground-based interceptor rockets, and the possibility that their deployment might lead irrevocably to abrogation of the ABM Treaty. While National Security Advisor Sandy Berger and his defense assistant Robert Bell struggled to find a means of deploying interceptors solely in North Dakota in order to preserve the treaty, the NRO and Space Command were pushing full speed ahead with space plans that reinforced a style of dominance that would be relied upon in theaters ranging from Kosovo to Colombia.

While one element of the *Vision for 2020* document of 1996 called for 'Global Partnerships,' such partial nods to multilateralism took a back seat to the call for 'Control of Space,' and the related mission of 'Global Engagement.' On the space control front, Space Command now was claiming for the US the sole right to maintain 24-hour reconnaissance of the planet from space. All use of space by US government agencies, or by companies allied with US interests, was talked about in terms of assured access, while the utilization of space by nations unfriendly to the US was to be met by what Space Command referred to as the 'Five D's: Destroy, Disrupt, Delay, Degrade, Deny.' Upon leaving the Space Command in 1996, Gen. Joseph Ashy made his famous comment that 'It's politically sensitive, and it isn't in vogue, but, absolutely, we're going to fight in space. We're going to fight from space, and we're going to fight into space.'

The Global Engagement mission listed in the *Vision* document tied these space-usage strategies to precision weapons, as well as to intelligence. Space Command called for 'information dominance' through constant use of global surveillance capabilities; an operational missile defense to deny others the use of space; and precision strike weapons to make sure that responses to any regional skirmishes could be instantaneous and devastating. In practice, it would take the Clinton administration several quarters, or virtually to the end of its time in office, to fully meet the rhetoric Space Command put forth in 1996's *Vision*, and in the more detailed 1998 *Long-Range Plan*. But the blueprint was in place that later served the Bush administration's 2002 *National Security Strategy* so well.

The NRO's mission officially turned to information superiority with the August 1996 release of the Jeremiah Panel report, commissioned by acting NRO Director Keith Hall. Many concrete changes would await the conclusion of a larger federal commission on the NRO, which released its study in November 2000, but the real change in consciousness, involving the NRO supporting warfighting models, can be tied to the Jeremiah Report.[5] As part of the program to reform the NRO following the 1995–96 fiscal scandals, the Pentagon put in place a new office of the National Security Space Architect, a Defense Department official who could oversee missions of the NRO and the Defense Information Systems Agency. Robert Dickman was named to the post in 1996. The office drew up a National Space Policy Document, which integrated Defense Space Policy, Intelligence Space Policy, and National Security Policy. Meanwhile, NRO itself created a new Office of Military Support to allow NRO agents to go directly into the battlefield with US military groups.

This decision did not find universal acceptance among NRO staff, particularly among the old-timers familiar with the agency serving only the national civilian authority. Six years after Hall put tactical distribution on a faster track, Gen. John Jumper, chief of staff of the Air Force under the Bush administration, joked that 'the very thought of an NRO signal coming down and being accessed by anyone other than an NRO tribal representative is unthinkable to some.'[6]

Additional satellite platforms were orbited during this time, critical in completing the Space Command vision. Milstar, for example, was a notorious and over-priced satellite conceived during the Reagan administration for providing continued low-data-rate communications in the UHF and EHF bands, even after the initiation of a nuclear war. The original two Milstar-1 satellites were launched into geosynchronous orbit in 1994 and 1995. In the meantime, however, Milstar was redesigned in 1990 to emphasize higher data-rates and less nuclear survivability. The Milstar-2, the design of which was finished following the end of the Cold War, was intended for tactical missions. The first of this second generation was launched in April 1999, but a poor attitude-control software program led to a total loss of the satellite. Successful launches were carried out in January 2002, November 2002, and April 2003, however. The successor to Milstar-2, informally dubbed Milstar-3, is the Advanced Extremely High Frequency satellite. A national team of Hughes, Lockheed-Martin, and TRW was chosen to develop the satellite in April 2000. AEHF, also called Pathfinder, is expected to commence with launches in fiscal 2006.

Meanwhile, the results of the Space Warfare Center's Project Strike had been used to design the ultimate in space-based intelligence-distribution systems, the Global Broadcast System. The first public demonstration of the GBS prototype occurred at the 1996 National Space Symposium in Colorado Springs. Utilizing dedicated transceivers on the Navy's UHF Follow-On satellite, GBS provided one-way broadcasts of information ranging from open CNN broadcasts to closed sources such as the NSA's Binocular intelligence database, traffic from the Secret IP Router Network (SIPRNET), and messages from the Defense Department's top-secret Proteus Asynchronous Transfer Mode switching network. Speeds in the asymmetric system ranged from 160 Kbits/sec in a secondary channel, to more than 1 Mbit/sec in primary feed, though users' anecdotal stories suggest that streaming video was far choppier than residential civilian users might experience from a cable-TV or Digital Subscriber Line modem. A few rudimentary terminals for GBS were positioned in Bosnia and Hungary for use by the Bosnia peacekeeping teams, and terminals were more widely disseminated in the months following the NATO bombardment of Kosovo in 1999. By the time virtual bases were created around Colombia as part of Plan Colombia in 2000, GBS was a regular feature of the landscape wherever US troops were deployed.

The stampede to space had a significant effect on the high end of launch capability. Of more than 15 Titan-IV launches (and unsuccessful launch attempts) at Cape Canaveral and Vandenberg Air Force Base from 1989 to 2002, only one mission, NASA's nuclear-powered Cassini mission, was an open civilian mission. All others were military, the vast majority consisting of completely deniable launches of SIGINT satellites such as Trumpet, Mercury, Mentor, and Crystal. With Lockheed-Martin putting an end-of-life stop on Titan-IV production early in the twenty-first century, NRO anxiously promoted funding for both the Delta-IV and Atlas-5 launch vehicles, designed by Boeing and Lockheed-Martin, respectively. These two rockets were funded under the Evolved Expendable Launch Vehicle program, which sought to reduce the heavy costs of the Titan-IV by using cheaper components and streamlined design methods. Both EELV rockets offered less lift than the Titan-IV, requiring satellite manufacturers to eke out every possible advantage from electronics miniaturization.

The final military engagements of the Clinton administration spotlight the continued evolution of these space methodologies. For the twin assaults on Sudan and Afghanistan in August 1998, the cruise missile was king. Laser-guided weapons took too long, and required too much prepositioning, while cheap bombs guided by GPS navigational satellites were not ready. Similarly, the Desert Fox campaign of December 1998, in which the US and UK tried to prod Saddam Hussein to resume inspections on the basis of massive bombing, was more a macho display than a live experiment of space capabilities. The December campaign seemed so directly tied to Clinton's impeachment hearings over the Monica Lewinsky scandal, it was referred to privately by military commanders not as Desert Fox, but as Free Willy.

When Operation Allied Force, challenging Milosevic's policy in Kosovo, began in March 1999, the will to use overwhelming precision force was not there. While Madeleine Albright had talked tough to Serb representatives at the February 1999 negotiations in Rambouillet, France, many in the administration were well aware that the Kosovo Liberation Army, infused with terrorists and drug dealers, had played a provocative role in encouraging Serb 'cleansing' operations through vicious attacks on Serb forces. US and British representatives prodded NATO into proceeding with bombing without a UN Security Council resolution, but there was reticence on both Pentagon and State Department sides, giving rise to a target list that was severely restricted. During early phases of the bombing, more than 160 cruise missiles once again took center stage, with 100

Tomahawks fired from sea, and 60 air-launched cruise missiles fired from bombers.

The sea change in Kosovo bombing effectiveness came during NATO's fiftieth anniversary celebration in late April, when British Prime Minister Tony Blair urged an extremely aggressive campaign with ground troops, and NATO members were prodded into approving more aggressive aerial bombing. Some laser-guided bombs already had been used on hardened targets in Kosovo, and later in Belgrade, but the B-2 bomber, utilizing the Joint Direct Attack Munition (JDAM), became the star of the show. B-2 bombers were flown directly from Whiteman Air Force Base in Missouri to Kosovo, in single-day missions. They flew only 3 per cent of missions, but were responsible for more than 33 per cent of the targets hit. The primary weapon for the B-2 was the JDAM, of which more than 650 were dropped on Serb targets.

The JDAM may have been considered only 'semi-precise,' but it showed the power of the GPS navigational network. The idea originated with Air Force Chief of Staff Merrill McPeak in 1991, and a contract was awarded to Boeing in 1995. The basic concept was to use the existing inventory of Mk-82/83/84 bombs and BLU-109 penetrator bombs, and create a retrofit kit to give the bombs the power of GPS. Body strakes are added to the sides of the bomb, and a GPS navigator and tail fins are added to the rear. After the bomb is dropped from an aircraft, it spends 30 seconds in free-fall as GPS signals are acquired. The coordinates are provided to a subsystem called the Inertial Measurement Unit, which sends data to the autopilot of the bomb. The bomb is sent directly to its target, with an accuracy of 40 feet, using the tail fins. Halberstam, in his Kosovo study, said that 'purists now referred to this as an example of aerospace power, not air power, because of the importance of aerospace technology derived from satellites.' Once the JDAM had been proven, a variety of GPS-enabled bombs were ordered for Afghanistan and beyond, including the Wind-Corrected Munitions Dispenser from Lockheed-Martin, the Joint Standoff Weapon from Raytheon, and the Joint Air-to-Surface Standoff Missile from Lockheed-Martin. The Air Force and Navy now have at least 250,000 JDAMs on order, and a Boeing plant in St. Charles, Missouri was expected to increase production to 2,800 a month by late 2003.

A new platform experiencing its coming-of-age in Kosovo was based on technologies dating from World War II. The Unpiloted Aerial Reconnaissance Vehicle, or UAV, had reached a certain stage of maturity in the 1980s, but was ready for a quantum leap as military contractors applied advanced microprocessors and autonomous sensing subsystems to the basic UAV architecture. Early in the Clinton administration, a special dedicated Defense Department office had been created to oversee tactical intelligence flights of the U-2, SR-71, and smaller planes. The Defense Airborne Reconnaissance Office, or DARO, did not have a long life in the budget-strapped 1990s, but in 1994, it released a special study on Integrated Airborne Reconnaissance Strategy. This gave contractors such as Northrop-Grumman and General Atomics guidance on developing the next generation of UAV. Simpler UAVs, including TRW's Hunter, the IAI/TRW Pioneer, and the Bombardier/Dornier QL-289, required constant remote management from a ground-based human 'pilot.' The newer low-altitude Predator from General Atomics could be operated almost completely autonomously, and Northrop-Grumman promised even greater things for the high-altitude Global Hawk, when testing was completed at decade's end.

In the latter stages of the Bosnia operation, a limited number of Predators were sent to Taszar Air Base in Hungary, and Gjader in Albania, to monitor Serb positions in the Bosnian countryside. They were used primarily for imaging intelligence, in both photographic and synthetic-aperture radar applications. The greatest achievement of the Bosnia Predator deployment was Predator links to the Joint-STARS 'deep strike' radar plane, a first for a UAV system.

Even before the NATO decision to bomb Kosovo in 1999, UAVs were pre-positioned in several locations around greater Serbia. At least eight Predators were sent to Tuzla Air Base in Bosnia, used for both Bosnia and Kosovo operations. Hunter UAVs were sent to Skopje, and later moved to Gjader along with Army Task Force Hawk. The Navy relied on Pioneer UAVs, launched from the USS *Ponce* in the Adriatic Sea off Montenegro, to track actions of the Yuglosav Navy.

Some analysts assume the role of UAVs in Kosovo to have been an unassailable 'force multiplier,' but Tim Ripley of *Defence Systems Daily* pointed out several problems with UAVs, in a

December 1999 study.[7] Only the Hunter and Predator could use the Global Broadcast System, so Navy UAVs and those from European contractors had to rely on delayed fax distribution of imaging information. At times, this led to mistaken identification of buses or tractors as Serb armored units. All UAV missions were run from the NATO Combined Air Operations Group headquarters at Dal Molin Air Base in Vicenza, Italy, which occasionally led to bottlenecks in GBS traffic.

Ripley points out additional problems attributed specifically to SACEUR commander Gen. Wesley Clark, a controversial figure throughout the Kosovo operation. Clark had GBS terminals at his office and home in Mons, Belgium, and Ripley quotes several divisional intelligence officers off the record, who claim that Clark often would cut off regular intelligence sorties in order to analyze areas that were of personal interest to the commander. This points out a general problem of tactical intelligence distribution, TENCAP, and the Global Broadcast System – a little knowledge can be a dangerous thing, if regional commanders overrule general intelligence planning with arbitrary and contradictory orders to change UAV or satellite monitoring missions.

UAVs also suffered high losses in Kosovo, with four of eight Predators in Tuzla lost, four of seven off the USS *Ponce* lost, and seven of fourteen Hunters in Skopje and Gjader lost. Part of the problem was the predictable flight path taken by an aircraft without a human pilot, making it easier to shoot down a UAV. Some was related to the susceptibility to jamming of both the communication links and the GPS navigational links on many UAVs. In April 2000, the Defense Department ordered additional Hunters and Predators to the area, along with 125 troops from a reconnaissance division in Heidelberg. This reflected both the desire to beef up UAV coverage, as well as a concern that conditions in Kosovo were deteriorating, with greater skirmishes between the KLA and Serb forces. In any event, contractors were notified to increase the anti-jamming capabilities of UAVs in the future, as well as their maneuverability.

The Bosnia and Kosovo missions provided some interesting lessons that could be adopted by the State Department, Defense Department, and specifically the Space Command in fighting the drug war. When Howard Air Base in Panama closed in 1999 as a consequence of the Canal treaties, the Defense Department had

Valid photo ID required for all returns, exchanges and to receive and redeem store credit. With a receipt, a full refund in the original form of payment will be issued for new and unread books and unopened music within 30 days from any Barnes & Noble store. Without an original receipt, a store credit will be issued at the lowest selling price. With a receipt, returns of new and unread books and unopened music from bn.com can be made for store credit. A gift receipt or exchange receipt serves as proof of purchase only.

Valid photo ID required for all returns, exchanges and to receive and redeem store credit. With a receipt, a full refund in the original form of payment will be issued for new and unread books and unopened music within 30 days from any Barnes & Noble store. Without an original receipt, a store credit will be issued at the lowest selling price. With a receipt, returns of new and unread books and unopened music from bn.com can be made for store credit. A gift receipt or exchange receipt serves as proof of purchase only.

Valid photo ID required for all returns, exchanges and to receive and redeem store credit. With a receipt, a full refund in the original form of payment will be issued for new and unread books and unopened music within 30 days from any Barnes & Noble store. Without an original receipt, a store credit will be issued at the lowest selling price. With a receipt, returns of new and unread books and unopened music from bn.com can be made for store credit. A gift receipt or exchange receipt serves as proof of purchase only.

neither the time nor the budget to build up alternative air bases to support drug interdiction (in reality, anti-guerilla) operations in Colombia as part of the Plan Colombia aid package. A joint planning group led by the Pentagon devised the concept of the 'Forward Operating Location,' or FOL, which later was adopted rather liberally for the Forward Operating Base model in Afghanistan at the end of 2001. The strategy behind the FOL was to use existing airports and small airfields and augment them with small UAV runways, portable antenna fields staffed with NSA/CSS personnel, and portable satellite terminals managed by Space Command groups. Private companies, such as MPRI Inc. and DynCorp (the latter acquired by Computer Sciences Corp. at the end of 2002), played a key role in allowing the military and intelligence agencies a certain level of deniability.

By the end of 1999, contracts had been signed for FOLs to be set up at the Comalapa International Airport in El Salvador; at the Eloy Alfaro International Airport in Manta, Ecuador; and at two island locations in the Netherlands Antilles: Reina Beatrix Airport on Aruba, and Hato International Airport on Curacao. Airfields were upgraded for airborne missions from P-3s, E-2s, E-3s, and various UAVs. Portable terminals for GBS and Defense Department UHF communications were moved in, and rudimentary radar networks were assembled. Simultaneously, the Defense Department funded the construction of an integrated radar and intelligence center, run by the Colombian armed forces, at Tres Esquinas. A Congressional visit to Tres Esquinas discovered that some of the private contractors from DynCorp and other firms were overseeing UAV flights on behalf of the State Department, rather than the Defense Department.

When a CNN team visited Tres Esquinas in mid-2000, they learned that more than a thousand Americans were distributed between the Colombian base and the four FOLs surrounding Colombia. Many of them were private contractors, allowing the Pentagon to claim that fewer than 400 military personnel were involved in Plan Colombia. Many were involved in classified signals intelligence flights, such as Senior Scout, a listening platform for a special version of a C-130 plane called Comfy Levi; and Guard Rail, a special secret signals intelligence mission using RC-12 flights linked via real-time terminals to Hunter Army Air Field in Savannah, Georgia.

This melding of private and federal resources was no fluke limited to Colombia alone. As part of Vice President Al Gore's program for reinventing government, 'outsourcing' to private industry had become the new buzzword throughout the intelligence community. For example, Raytheon Corp. had taken over the bulk of intelligence processing duties for the NRO/NSA operation at Buckley Air Force Base in Aurora, Colorado, using a massive facility adjacent to Buckley that also housed Raytheon's secure Web hosting operations for corporate customers. At many global NSA and NRO sites, efforts to 'go remote' by replacing personnel with automated computer and communication systems, had been followed by an outsourcing mission to turn collection and processing duties over to private companies.

The most intriguing and controversial case of outsourcing came in the use of commercial satellite systems to augment or replace NRO intelligence. For a brief period of years in the mid-1990s, private commercial satellite systems, as well as privatized launch facilities, were eclipsing official government programs. As part of the craze inspired by the Internet boom, coalitions of private companies often led by defense contractors, cobbled together low-earth orbit networks for high-resolution imaging, personal voice communications, and even broadband Internet communications. Indeed, military officials were grumbling during space symposia in mid-decade that the Iridium and Globalstar networks were grabbing all the venture-capital funding and all the glory.

When former NRO Director Jeff Harris landed at Space Imaging Inc. after leaving the agency, the NRO began to pay close attention to the issue of new commercial imaging satellites with resolution of a few meters. For a few brief quarters after his appointment, the new NRO Director Keith Hall talked of 'shutter control' – halting space imaging companies from providing certain images to a range of customers in the event of hostilities. And in fact, Congress even passed a bill to prevent sales of private images of Israel – one of the most egregious cases in the 1990s of the power of the Israel lobby in US government.

By 1999, however, Hall had done a complete about-face, touting the NRO's 'Commercial Imagery Initiative' in which the NRO would purchase a certain percentage of commercial images for use by the agency. By the time of the Afghanistan invasion, the NRO was snapping up all available commercial images from the leading private imagery suppliers, achieving a form of censorship through the free market that did not raise the controversy that might be caused by any mandated 'shutter control.' Brig. Gen. Brian Arnold, director of requirements at the Air Force Space Command, said in a 1999 speech that the Space Warfare Center at Schriever had begun a Special Project '99 with the NRO and the National Imagery and Mapping Agency, under which commercial and government imaging data would be fused into a seamless whole, which could then be distributed via GBS in a manner similar to the Talon programs.

Private low-earth orbit (LEO) communication satellites largely became a non-issue, as investors quickly discovered that the proliferation of terrestrial cellular phone networks made space-based networks like Iridium and Globalstar the kind of gold-plated, expensive networks with oversized telephone handsets that few people, even upper-class executives, required. As the Internet economy crashed and burned in mid-2000, it took the LEO communications industry down with it. Motorola, prime contractor for Iridium, even announced it would de-orbit the Iridium satellites already in orbit and shut down the system, until the Defense Department joined a consortium that found some tangential uses for a truncated, limited Iridium system that remained in existence with joint commercial and military duties.

As is often the case, privatization brought corruption and security fears in its wake. This was nowhere more evident than in the flap over the transfer of satellite and rocket information from Hughes Electronic Systems, and Loral Space and Communications in the mid-1990s. Neo-conservatives, in particular the alarmist Bill Gertz of the *Washington Times*, used the lever of corporate donations to the Clinton campaign by Loral and Hughes as prima-facie evidence of deliberate treasonous activities on the part of the Clinton administration. Gertz, in his *Times* articles on missile proliferation and his partisan book *Betrayal*, makes legitimate points about aerospace contractors aiding Chinese missile guidance, and about the tendency of pro-trade Clinton officials to ignore Chinese trade in missile technology to Pakistan and North Korea. What was deeply ironic in Gertz's conclusions was that conservatives were deeply involved in aid to contractors as well – Richard Perle, architect of the 2001 unilateralist drive, was involved in aiding Loral in hearings before the State Department, proving that bending the rules for large defense contractors was a bipartisan issue.

Yet, the mood at aerospace industry meetings in the late 1990s was more one of resentment at the State Department for tightening up technology transfers to other nations, than one of anger at Clinton for allowing security breaches in US space technology. This showcased the continuing breach between social conservatives and free-marketeers: All transnational companies, including military contractors, saw the advantages of enlarged markets as more important than the preservation of secure technologies controlled by the US. Those overly concerned with security, including not only Gertz and Rep. Curt Weldon, but even supposed arms-control advocates like Gary Milhollin of the Wisconsin Arms Control Project, found that their warnings of technology proliferation mostly fell on deaf ears. If there was a buck to be made, that was more important than keeping the lid on technology transfer. In practice, US technology was so far ahead of any other nation by the end of the Clinton era that the leaks that took place in the Hughes/Loral affair represented only small breaches in an otherwise seamless wall of US technology dominance.

This message carried little weight with the team around candidate George Bush, however. Incoming Defense Secretary Donald Rumsfeld served on two additional presidential commissions, providing reports immediately after the November 2000 elections and immediately following the Bush inauguration, which set the stage for the brash unilateralism that characterized the Bush presidency in the eight months preceding the September 11 al-Qaeda attacks.

8
'In Your Face From Outer Space'

Coincidence, of course, drove the release of the first two major presidential commission reports on military space during the tumultuous period between the contested 2000 elections and the inauguration of George W. Bush. Yet the two reports on the National Reconnaissance Office and on national security space policy served as bookends for the long transitional period preceding the arrival in office of the most blatantly unilateralist president in history.

Bush's promise to lead from the center was disproven as his cabinet was chosen, populated with many of the hard-line veterans of the Nixon, Ford, and Reagan years who had been responsible for the Committee on the Present Danger and the Heritage Foundation. Some analysts would point to the involvement of second-string Bush cabinet members, such as Richard Perle, Douglas Feith, and Paul Wolfowitz, in organizations like the Project for a New American Century, as proof of some dark and well-planned intent. While there was an element of truth in the sinister nature of the programs promoted by the Perle/Wolfowitz clique, the leaders of the Bush unilateralist program actually shared common membership in many organizations, and had many common visions, centered on ruling the planet through imperial dictum.

This was made evident as the Defense Department schemers inserted one of their own, John Bolton, under Colin Powell at the State Department. Bolton was a man who explicitly stated that the US government had no interest in signing or respecting treaties any longer, since a nation as powerful as the US should simply dictate terms to the other nations of the world. Clinton already had destroyed Kyoto, the International Criminal Court, and the ABM Treaty in all but name. The belief that Bush took the initiative to renounce these treaties ignores the extent to which his team was handed multiple *faits accomplis*. Yet it took brash opportunists like Bolton and the Defense Department clique to give a name to in-your-face braggadocio, thereby making clear to allies and adversaries alike just who was in charge.

The November 2000 'Commission for the Review of the National Reconnaissance Office,' though nominally bipartisan in being chaired by Bob Kerrey and Porter Goss, made no bones about specifying what the NRO needed to do. The commission was following up on the post-1996 efforts by NRO Director Keith Hall to reform acquisition at the agency by chairing the Jeremiah Panel, a team led by retired Adm. David Jeremiah that intended to improve procurement methods for the upcoming FIA 8X and Intruder satellite programs.[1]

The problems with the agency had begun when the elder Bush and Clinton began the process of declassification, the 2000 commission decided. Allowing critics to grasp the elements of NRO missions 'has aided terrorists and other adversaries,' the report stated, while making the NRO less innovative and risk-taking. The NRO Director also needed guidance directly from the President, the Secretary of Defense, and the Director of Central Intelligence, the report stated, to make the difficult choice between emphasizing tactical or strategic intelligence. The commission followed the lead of the Jeremiah Panel in insisting that the NRO was too important an agency to segment, by giving SIGINT missions to the NSA and imaging missions to the National Imagery and Mapping Agency (NIMA). Instead, the commission insisted, the NRO should retain all space-based missions. It also should improve its innovative practices by creating a top-secret Office of Space Reconnaissance within the agency, which would focus on long-range programs that would be nurtured cradle to grave, with opportunities for budget set-asides to insure programs were completed. The commission report was short on alarmist language, but it led from the assumption that the US should maintain a sole position in global reconnaissance from space.

On January 11, 2001, the 'Commission to Assess United States National Security Management and Organization,' chaired by Donald Rumsfeld, presented a report warning of the possibility of a 'Space Pearl Harbor' if the nation did not treat its space supremacy seriously.[2] Perhaps not entirely by accident, the report was released just as the Space Warfare Center was carrying out its first global space battle-management simulation game, Schriever

I, at the base for which the exercise was named. Schriever I had nothing to do with simulations of battles between X-ray laser stations in space, and everything to do with applying the lessons of Talon, TENCAP, and Forward Operating Locations on a global basis.

Some conservative analysts would look back in the aftermath of September 11 and call the commission's talk of a 'Space Pearl Harbor' prescient, were it not for the fact that low-tech terrorists exploiting security holes in an airline system have nothing to do with either space supremacy or missile defense. What the commission was asking the world to believe is that the nation that spent more on its military than all other nations put together, which retained the only global power-projection capabilities on Earth, and which had perfected precision warfare to the point that victory could come with virtually no casualties on the victor's side, expected to be blindsided in a Pearl-Harbor-style action. Certainly, Rumsfeld's earlier missile commission had shown that US analysts must be much more aware of advanced multi-stage rocket programs like North Korea's Taepodong II and India's Agni and Prithvi. But Pearl Harbor? The only nations that need fear a Pearl Harbor would be those on the potential receiving end of US wrath.

The commission made several calls for giving the NRO director double-duty as chief procurement officer for space, which the Bush administration followed to the letter. It also made recommendations on the relationship between Space Command and nuclear forces, which Bush chose to interpret in odd ways. Space Command already had taken over responsibility in 1999 for Defense Department-wide computer-defense and computer-attack missions, and was clearly expanding its existing management of strategic land-based missile forces to include overall nuclear war strategy. But some commission members were no doubt surprised in late 2002, when the Bush administration interpreted the commission recommendations to mean that Space Command should be merged into Strategic Command in Omaha.

Rumsfeld, though he nominally left the commission after being named to the Secretary of Defense post, took the lead in introducing the commission's work just prior to the Bush inauguration. He stressed that strategic space missions must have the president's direct attention, that the Defense Department and the intelligence community were in dire need of reorganization in order to emphasize space, and that war in space would be a virtual certainty in the years to come. The time to bring more engineers, scientists, and bureaucrats into national security space planning was now, Rumsfeld said.

Given the attention paid to space just prior to the inauguration, some analysts were startled to hear little about space dominance or missile defense during the first four months Bush was in office. In truth, Bush realized that revised versions of a 1999 Clinton deployment plan for missile defense might be the best one could hope for in the near term – the only issue remaining was how to treat the ABM Treaty and its limitations.

Clinton's team, in order to short-circuit Republican actions to trash the ABM Treaty, had proposed a plan to have 20 interceptor rockets at Fort Greely, Alaska by 2005, expanding to 100 rockets in 2007. The only definite X-band radar would be a facility adjacent to the Cobra Dane radar on the bleak wind-swept island of Shemya in the western Aleutians, Alaska. Early-warning radar at Clear, Alaska; Beale Air Force Base, California; Cape Cod, Massachusetts, Thule, Greenland; and Fylingdales, England were to receive UHF phased-array upgrades (their second in a decade, albeit not full X-band replacement). A second phase of this 1999 plan would have added a Maine or North Dakota site with 125 interceptors, and expanded the network to nine X-band radars in 2010.

Bradley Graham stresses that European opposition to the new ground-based missile defense did not begin with the harsh response to the Bush tour of 2001. When Clinton officials presented their plans at the end of 1999, NATO governments were highly skeptical. Though they recognized the intermediate-missile threat spelled out in the 1998 Rumsfeld Commission report, they believed that an appropriate analysis had to combine an examination of technical capability with an assessment of how hostile the state's behavior had been. John Holum, the head of arms control initiatives in the Clinton State Department, had been more candid than other officials in discussing Russia's concerns about the SBIRS-Low satellite in the past. Graham, in his *Hit to Kill* book, credits Holum with another candid observation regarding the real concern over rogue states. Those in favor of missile defense were not so concerned about recalcitrant nations actually using nukes, Graham said, but about their utilizing 'operational weapons of coercive diplomacy to complicate US decision-making, or limit our freedom to act.' In other words, US decision-makers had the right to prevent any other state from behaving as it wished, but no other state should carry any potential capability to limit the US's power-projection capabilities. The asymmetry of unilateralism already was fully subscribed to in the Clinton administration by the time the 1999 decision was discussed with allies.

Vladimir Putin's government encouraged an attitude of skepticism regarding the mix of missile defense and precision weapons, and relations were made worse in the last year of the Clinton administration, after Congress rejected the Comprehensive Test Ban Treaty. After multiple reports revealing skyrocketing costs of search-radar construction, and the failure of two interceptor tests in early 2000, Clinton decided in September 2000 to defer any construction decisions, which in effect pushed construction starts on the Shemya X-band radar out to 2002. Clinton also passed at the last minute on a personal meeting with Kim Jong Il of North Korea to discuss intermediate-range missiles, deciding that pushing for a final Israel–Palestine settlement at Taba (a meeting that came to naught prior to the election of Ariel Sharon) was more important in his administration's last days than a North Korea meeting of dubious value.

When Bush came to office, he immediately put further negotiations with North Korea on ice. To the surprise of some missile-defense critics, he did not immediately push for weapons deployment, either. Rumsfeld discussed a modified Alaska interceptor program, in which a pseudo-civilian space launch facility on Kodiak Island would take the place of launching missiles directly from Fort Greely, while Shemya was kept on hold in favor of more upgrades to the Clear, Alaska radar site.

The more important element in missile defense for the Bush team was not the deployment details of the interceptors and radar, but the explicit renunciation of ABM. The first strong indicator that the 1972 treaty mattered little to the professional treaty busters came in a May 1, 2001 speech at the National Defense University, where Bush questioned the very purpose of ABM.

Rumsfeld's team spent the bulk of the spring and summer working on the Quadrennial Defense Review (QDR) and Nuclear Posture Review (NPR), a mandated analysis of where US defense policy was headed. In the highly charged atmosphere following September 11, much was made of the nations explicitly named in the NPR – Iran, Iraq, Libya, North Korea, Syria, China – and the fact that this administration was more likely than ever before to cross the 'firebreak' between conventional and nuclear weapons. In reality, the Bush NPR was merely a more explicit spelling-out of the same assumptions and constraints that had driven mainstream Republican and Democrat nuclear-warfare thinking since the end of the Cold War.

What was most significant was Rumsfeld's introductory observation in the unclassified executive summary for the NPR that a 'New Triad' had replaced the old Cold War Triad of bombers, ICBMs, and SLBMs. The first leg of offensive weapons included all the elements of the old triad, augmented by precision conventional weapons, which the NPR counted as every bit as significant to global warfare as strategic nukes. The second leg of the new triad included defenses, both active and passive; while the third leg was comprised of infrastructure, including intelligence and communications.

The NPR assumed that a viable strategic arsenal in 2012 could be comprised of between 1,700 and 2,000 nuclear weapons, distributed among 14 Trident submarines, 500 Minuteman III land-based missiles, 76 B-52H bombers, and 21 B-2 bombers. Significant upgrades in infrastructure would include the Advanced Wideband System to replace the Advanced EHF satellite; and a fuzzily-defined 'system of systems' for intelligence, combining space, air, sea, and land assets, a network sounding like an augmented GBS distribution system combined with enhanced imaging and signals interception from space.

The second leg also was left largely to the imagination in the NPR. Basic assumptions on missile defense seemed centered on the renunciation of the ABM Treaty, which was not made manifest until 2002. Beyond that, the NPR mentioned a rudimentary ground-based interceptor system, the centerpiece of Bush's announced 2002 missile-defense strategy; sea-based theater missile defense, later reduced to theater-wide Aegis-only systems as the Area Missile Defense system of the Navy was deemed too costly; and some possible operational use of the Airborne Laser, an assumption later called into questions by testing problems in late 2002 and early 2003. In short, it was good for the administration that the Missile Defense Agency later called for fielding systems without exhaustive testing. The Bush administration was faced with the same problem as its predecessor: the rush to deploy missile-defense weapons could not change the fact that nothing was viable yet.

While the interlude was quickly forgotten in the aftermath of terror attacks, it is worth remembering how the Defense Department was in apparent disarray in the summer of 2001. Both QDR and NPR were facing tough going in a US Senate that had shifted to a Democratic majority with the defection of Republican Sen. James Jeffords to the Democratic Party. Bush's June tour of NATO nations and Russia, in which he tried to justify ABM abrogation, went so poorly that Rumsfeld made a follow-up trip to Moscow in mid-August to explain why missile defense was good for everyone. A few short weeks later, the time spent in damage control appeared largely irrelevant.

There was nothing surprising about the cries for expanded missile defense and more aggressive intelligence that arose within hours of the attacks on the World Trade Center and the Pentagon on September 11. While the success of small-group terror attacks using low-technology weapons would seem to represent the antithesis of an expected rogue-state missile launch, the public was not ready to make those distinctions, and neither was Congress. By September 15, any gambler could guess that missile defense would gain its full requested $8.3 billion for the next fiscal year, that intelligence spending would be increased across the board in both technical and 'HUMINT' realms, and that something akin to the USA Patriot Act would sail through Congress with scarcely a dissenting voice. The sobering aspect was how long the fallout from September 11 tainted honest analysis of the war on terror: anti-war demonstrations may have reached massive size when the US turned from direct targets in 2002 to pre-emptive war in 2003, but legislative, executive, and judicial branches alike remained locked in a model of a repressive state wearing a new unilateral mantle in the guise of a moral crusade.

Paul Wolfowitz set the tone for the new supremacy on September 13, when he called for 'ending states' that supported terrorism. This obviously applied to Afghanistan, where the Taliban provided explicit support for Osama bin Laden's al-Qaeda organization, but many members of Bush's inner cabinet were convinced that it should also apply to the nations later referred to as the 'axis of evil,' as well as a few other assorted bad-guys. Bush's simultaneous call to be either 'with us or with the terrorists' set the tenor for leaders on the periphery of Afghanistan, like Musharraf in Pakistan. Full help in terms of both military basing and police work must be provided to the new American crusaders, or states on the fence would surely fall.

An open-ended mission extending beyond an assault on Afghanistan was favored by Wolfowitz and Rumsfeld long before the president's 2002 State of the Union address. Within a week of the attacks, Defense Department teams were calling for attacks on both Iraq, and on Hezbollah groups in the Bekaa Valley of Lebanon, despite the lack of any evidence tying the organizations to al-Qaeda. Gen. Ralph 'Ed' Eberhart, commander of the US Space Command and future head of Northern Command, was playing a crucial role within the first week of preparation for Operation Enduring Freedom. Eberhart told Eric Schmitt of the *New York Times* on September 26 that he had been given authority by Vice President Cheney to assign two generals, Gen. Norton Schwartz and Gen. Larry Arnold, the duty of downing commercial jets deemed to be a threat, without seeking specific civilian authority.

The Space Command also was key to the rapid buildup of forces surrounding Afghanistan at the end of September and beginning of October. Because of pre-positioning of equipment in Diego Garcia and at Prince Sultan Air Base in Saudi Arabia, the US was able to bring force levels to 30,000 troops before the month of September was over. The model of the Colombian Forward Operating Locations was adopted, first at existing bases at Camp Doha in Kuwait and Fifth Fleet Headquarters in Bahrain, and later at rapidly expanding bases in the former Soviet republics in Central Asia. Several covert groups of Green Berets and CIA teams had been in Uzbekistan since 1999 in order to fight the Islamic Movement of Uzbekistan, making the expansion of covert insertion teams to Afghanistan proper a relatively straightforward task. In the final days leading up to the October 7 air assault, a thousand troops from the 10th Mountain Division were sent to Khanabad and Tuzel, Uzbekistan, and several AWACS and KC-135 planes were pre-positioned at Masirah Air Base in Oman. A few days earlier, Bush had approved tens of millions of dollars of covert CIA funds going to Northern Alliance groups in Afghanistan.

The biggest bottleneck came in airborne technical equipment to support the assault. Of the $4.2 billion in emergency spending sought by the Defense Department following September 11, almost $1.4 billion was aimed at intelligence programs, in particular ramping prototyping up to production for the high-altitude, long-range Global Hawk UAV, and expanding production of RC-135V Rivet Joint reconnaissance aircraft. Northrop Grumman's Global Hawk was still in a very early shipping phase, with only six such aircraft having been sent to the field. The Predator, for 600-mile lower-altitude flights, had proven its capability in Bosnia, but only seven of a total inventory of 40 were in the region in late September, split between the Air Force and CIA. Predator contractor General Atomics, however, had very little leeway in accelerating production, regardless of new emergency funding coming in. General Atomics had an easier job producing a small, dedicated UAV for the CIA, a 24-foot robot plane called the Gnat, intended for radar reconnaissance using the Lynx radar system. Combining the Gnat with covert special operations crews inserted into Afghanistan, allowed the CIA to gain moving-target indicator capability which could be fed into GBS information for tactical military groups.

Tallying UAV use in Afghanistan was no easy task, due to the CIA and Air Force being somewhat reticent to talk about numbers acquired and deployed. The widespread and outsourced use of UAVs had been demonstrated in Colombia, where many UAV operations were managed directly by the State Department, or directly by DynCorp, MPRI, and similar contractors on behalf of government agencies. This aided CIA deniability, in the same way that Air America and other proprietary corporations operated on behalf of the CIA in Vietnam. The CIA was anxious to demonstrate the use of UAVs armed with Hellfire missiles, the so-called Unpiloted Combat Aerial Vehicles, or UCAVs. The

Predator/Hellfire configuration may have been a bit of a retrofit, but soon after the end of the Afghanistan fighting, Boeing Corp. was testing a UCAV designed specifically for combat, the X-45, using technology from a Boeing test stealth aircraft developed in the 1990s called 'Bird of Prey.'[3]

President Bush's loosened restrictions on assassination missions allowed UCAVs to be targeted directly at individuals in al-Qaeda, though the legal skirmishes over targets led to the failure of a UCAV mission on October 7, when an assault on Taliban leader Mullah Muhammad Omar was not approved in time to assault the sheikh. Originally the CIA had claimed responsibility for assaulting individual terrorist groups, while the Pentagon had responsibility for direct Taliban units. Sorting out this level of responsibility led to a delay on October 7 that allowed Omar to get away. This drove the White House into loosening UCAV rules of engagement still further at the end of the year, first allowing a Predator to be used in successfully targeting Mohammed Atef, a key al-Qaeda operative, on November 15, and eventually driving the successful pre-emptive UCAV attack on al-Qaeda in November 2002.

The October 7 air assaults on Afghanistan made no immediate use of such small-scale tools, however. The 'softening-up' of Afghan rudimentary air defense was carried out by cruise missiles, and by B-2 aircraft carrying JDAMs, which arrived in the area from Whiteman Air Force Base, but which returned to Diego Garcia for local basing.

From the first day of conflict, space played an important role in Operation Enduring Freedom. Peter Teets, the former chief operating officer of Lockheed-Martin, had taken over in the combined role of NRO director, under-secretary of the Air Force, and chief procurement officer for space. Because Keith Hall had stayed on until April 2001 as NRO director, and the White House had been slow to name a successor, Teets had only been on the job mere weeks prior to the September 11 attacks. Yet he proved capable of managing a military space budget which Teets himself estimated at $68 billion a year.

Teets expanded Hall's commercial imaging program by working with the National Imagery and Mapping Agency to buy up virtually all the commercial imagery products available from the Space Imaging Inc. Ikonos satellite. The NRO and NIMA also acquired large amounts of Spot Image and QuickBird images. Under the Space Imaging deal, NIMA paid $1.9 million a month for Ikonos access, and $20 a square kilometer for images actually purchased. News agencies and commercial groups could only gain access to those Ikonos images approved by the Pentagon.

By acquiring all Space Imaging products on the open market, the Pentagon avoided the political hassle of censoring commercial imagery products from space. In June 2002, CIA Director George Tenet went a step further in declaring Space Imaging and DigitalGlobe to be the primary mapping satellite systems for the waning war in Afghanistan. By assigning commercial imaging satellites a general mapping role, the CIA and NIMA could dedicate national satellites to special close-look tasks. In addition, Teets relied upon the new administrator at NASA, Sean O'Keefe, who had a military background in the US Navy before joining NASA. O'Keefe was happy to provide the Pentagon with images from specialized satellites such as SeaWiFS and Terra. The tight links between Teets and O'Keefe would later be solidified with a communications agency that linked the NRO, Space Command, and NASA.

The Defense Department's rationale in acquiring an interest in the bankrupt low-earth orbit commercial satellite network, the Iridium system designed by Motorola, was not immediately apparent at the time of Enduring Freedom. But the Special Forces announced soon after the war was over that they would use a new handheld computer, Joint Expeditionary Digital Information or JEDI, which would combine an Iridium phone, GPS transponder, laser range-finder, and text messaging system in a Palmtop using the Window CE operating system. This way, the ground laser-targeting task performed by special forces could be integrated into GPS, Iridium, and eventually GBS networks.

In order to accelerate distribution of GPS coordinates for use by JDAM bombs, UCAVs, and aircraft with dumb bombs, Air Force Space Command initiated the GPS Enhanced Theatre Support program, or GETS, which put GPS coordinates for smart bombs on a fast track. Teets said during a space conference in the spring of 2002 that the Global Broadcast System was relied upon heavily in the early days of the war. Using a Navy UHF Follow-On satellite parked above Diego Garcia, the GBS relayed instant video feeds from Predator UAVs to CIA insertion teams who were riding on horseback, distributing money and material to Northern Alliance forces, all the while utilizing video intelligence transferred down to battery-powered laptops which the CIA agents took with them in-country. 'We, in Space Command, provided Tommy Franks seven times the bandwidth that was provided to Norman Schwarzkopf, and an individual soldier had 322 times the bandwidth that was available in Desert Storm,' Space Command head Ed Eberhart said in April 2002. 'In no time in our history has the capability of space been so pivotal.'

Special Operations soldiers were critical in enabling the fall of the northern city of Mazar-i-Sharif for a very obvious reason. Nearly twenty years of Soviet occupation, followed by three years of brutal and primitive Taliban rule, had reduced Afghanistan's infrastructure to veritable medieval bare minimum. Within four days of the initial B-2 assaults, bombers were scaling back large-scale missions because there was little left to bomb in terms of large air-defense systems, communication networks, or power grids. Instead, air forces had to wait for special operations troops to call in laser-guided assaults on individual clusters of Taliban regular forces, al-Qaeda fighters, and international 'volunteers' who had come to fight the American infidels. All of these special assaults were enabled using space, and they were all the Air Force had left to do by mid-October.

Nevertheless, by early November an advance Pentagon team was touring three former air bases in Tajikistan (Khudjand, Kurgan-Tyube, and Kolyab), as well as facilities in Kyrgyzstan and Kazakhstan, to prepare for support of eventual US bases in Mazar-i-Sharif, Kabul, and Kandahar. The strategy borrowed heavily from the Colombian FOL model, using specialized space troops to bring in support for portable antenna fields and GBS terminals.

Many short-term skeptics of US progress in October were startled at the rapid collapse of the Taliban in the latter half of November. There was nothing surprising about the disintegration of resistance, however. With all infrastructure destroyed in the first week of bombing, and ground forces within the country calling in air strikes on larger formations of troops and civilians in early November, there was nothing left to a Taliban organization by the third week of November. The establishment of a semi-permanent air base at Bagram Air Base allowed the US to completely dominate all air space in the region. Once the

Marines had established a base southwest of Kandahar for orchestrating integrated air and ground assaults, there was little left but mop-up operations deep within the southern mountains.

It is easy to point to the limitations of the Forward Operating Base strategy, and to the limitations of using precision bombing and remote robots in rugged mountain terrain, when examining the results of the Tora Bora and Anaconda operations in December and March. In reality, the operations showed both the unprecedented power of war from space, and the limitations – both operational and moral. Small teams of US soldiers were able to pinpoint attacks to small canyons and cave complexes in a vast region on the Afghanistan–Pakistan border. But is it such a surprise that the US could not bring home the grand prizes of Osama Bin Laden and Mohammed Omar? NSA Director Michael Hayden had warned several months prior to the start of the war that the operational security practiced by both al-Qaeda and the Taliban, and the caution Bin Laden had used in making both terrestrial and low-earth-orbit wireless phone calls, showed that the powers of the NSA were not omnipotent. When a small group of individual actors can move freely in a vast region populated by sympathetic civilians, no amount of high-tech intelligence can provide an infallible guarantee of targeting the small group.

Stephen Biddle of the Army War College's Strategic Studies Institute, in an analysis of the later battles against Taliban and al-Qaeda remnants, says that such decentralized groups should not be considered the equivalent of guerilla operators similar to the Vietcong. A dedicated battle group can keep up moderate-sized formations and still remain relatively immune to modern intelligence techniques. Biddle suggested in a 2003 *Foreign Affairs* article that small groups which use effective ground cover and maintain radio silence, can keep themselves hidden from imaging and signals satellites, and to some extent even from next-generation infrared and radar. Space intelligence does indeed ease the task for ground forces, Biddle concluded, but massive use of standoff weapons cannot win all wars. This is an indicator of why the Anaconda mountain battles were so difficult, and why Bin Laden was able to get into Pakistan.[4]

Biddle's analysis also had a lot to say about the ground battle in Iraq. Space intelligence and standoff precision weapons excel in destroying centralized infrastructure. They can make a state or a liberation group grow brittle, allowing for quick collapses of central authority as seen in Kunduz and Kabul in November 2001, and in Baghdad in April 2003. Dedicated groups can remain somewhat immune from the power of omniscient intelligence, albeit for short periods of time if they are not mobile. Over a longer period of time, such 'total situational awareness' can make a victory against individual actors all but assured, in the same way that the FBI sooner or later finds most fugitives that have not left US territory. As is often the case, Congressional leaders who launched probes of NSA and CIA activities in Enduring Freedom were asking the wrong questions: The important issue was not finding out why Bin Laden was not yet in custody, but specifying how many freedoms US citizens were willing to give up, and how blatant a security net US agencies could throw over the rest of the world, in order to make terror-hunting operations operate more effectively in a short period of time.

Overwhelming war plans with lopsided kill ratios also created deep moral issues, even for the most callous of military leaders in the US. Officers, from Gen. Tommy Franks on down, began asking, first in private but later in official academic military journals, whether the US military could operate in 'honorable' fashion with such an asymmetric advantage over the rest of the world. These questions rarely intruded upon the visions of the civilian leadership. Politicians from both parties figured that if an overwhelming advantage in intelligence and firepower could allow the US to dominate any venue on the planet's surface, the morality of the operation could be judged by the absence of body bags. Of course, as the failure to report Afghan casualties in the US media showed, collateral damage involving civilians on the other side simply was not an issue. To be fair, precision weapons kept the casualty numbers lower than they might otherwise have been. But political leaders, mainstream media, and the American people themselves put forth the message that if fewer American soldiers died in practicing planetary dominance, no other issues need be considered. This was the moral background that allowed the war on terror to morph in 2002–03 into a permanent war on the rest of the planet.

9
Permanent War

The drivers for renouncing the ABM Treaty and for extending the 'war on terror' to Iraq and beyond shared a common base that often went unrecognized. Rather than search for a mysterious and cryptic cause in organizations like the Defense Policy Board, it is simpler to recognize the view, driving Rumsfeld and his underlings, that deterrence played no role in a world driven by failed states and unstable non-state actors. (While deterrence and the Mutually Assured Destruction theory obviously have a questionable moral validity when a nuclear state confronts a non-nuclear one, the argument relevant to the Bush Doctrine is that deterrence's absence represented an even more horrific scenario.) If deterrence was useless, then obviously missile defense would have to be deployed quickly and widely, in both regional theaters and national venues. If deterrence was useless, then containing dangerous leaders who would not pay the US proper fealty simply would not work. Their nations would have to be attacked and defeated, one by one, in the Rumsfeld view of the world. The realization of how far the anti-deterrence crowd was willing to go did not dawn on many allies and critics of the Bush administration until the 2002 State of the Union Address put final notice on the so-called 'axis of evil.'

But the signs were there for those who chose to pay attention, as early as Bush's speech to the United Nations in October 2001. He played upon several of the themes he would reiterate nearly a year later, when he demanded UN action against Iraq in his September 12 UN speech. Given where rhetoric was taking the Bush cabinet, the US Congress should have been extremely cautious at giving Bush *carte blanche* on extending the war beyond Afghanistan, and equally cautious about giving Attorney General John Ashcroft more power under the USA Patriot Act. Instead, members of Congress asked why the act could not be more effective in quashing civil liberties. Leaders from both parties joined with jingoistic newspaper columnists in demanding direct attacks on Iraq, long before the Taliban was chased out of Kandahar. Is it any wonder that the trajectory of events laying waste to international treaties and validating first-strike war was so disappointingly predictable between early 2002 and the invasion of Iraq in March 2003?

Perhaps part of the reason the 'attack Iraq' rhetoric became so harsh so quickly was due to the degree to which Vladimir Putin and the Russian elite, as well as the party leaders in China, both pulled back from their anti-BMD tirades of 2001. China was tempered in its actions in the UN by the lure of joining the World Trade Organization, but it was difficult to figure out Putin's motivation. Given Putin's belated decision to join with France and Germany in early 2003 against the Iraq war, why was he willing to adopt Bush's view of an informal, non-codified reduction in nuclear weapons? Why did he fold so easily on ABM Treaty abrogation? Those too jaded to believe that it was simply a matter of George Bush's charm point to possible quid pro quos involving the Russian actions against Chechen rebels, in both Chechnya and in the Pankisi Gorge in Georgia. Certainly Bush's criticism of the October 2002 Moscow police use of a fentanyl gas during the theater hostage crisis was muted. But there was more going on behind the scenes.

Russia's equivalent of the NSA, the FAPSI, was all but deteriorating in the new century. In October 2001, after insisting for years that the Lourdes, Cuba FAPSI electronic intelligence base would stay open in any event, Putin announced its eventual closure in a highly-publicized event. This came not long after the last Russian naval signals intelligence antennas had been closed at Cam Ranh Bay, Vietnam. By the end of the year, US officials began scouting around the West African island nation of Sao Tome e Principe for antenna sites, hoping to use a former GRU/FAPSI site located there. As US relations with Yemen began to improve in early 2002, Defense Department officials began examining another former FAPSI site on the island of Socotra, hoping to make it a key US forward-operating post for the Iraq war to come. Perhaps this was simply a case of new tenants moving into a property that had proved its worth with past occupants. Or perhaps there were elements of a Bush–Putin 'understanding' that have yet to come to light. The gentlemen's agreement to wink at the ABM Treaty's demise, however, appeared to be falling apart in the spring of 2003, a victim of Putin's exasperation over the US's hard line on Iraq.

This double standard also applied to France in the tense weeks leading up to the attack on Iraq. Since President Jacques Chirac represented some of the most conservative interests in the French policy elite, there was little argument to providing small CIA teams special access to French military facilities in Djibouti, on the Red Sea. The Hellfire missile that killed al-Qaeda members in Yemen in November 2002 came from a UCAV launched from Djibouti. Even as US–French relations soured in the spring of 2003, though, and the US Congress was renaming French fries served in the House cafeteria 'Freedom Fries,' Marines and Air Force personnel were heading to Djibouti to establish permanent facilities adjacent to the French base. This was the common sight throughout South Asia as the US prepared for battle.

In a mirror-image counterpoint to the Russian shrinkage of foreign bases, US offshore facilities were expanding faster than critics could follow them. New Central Asian bases like Manas in Kyrgyzstan were expanding despite the winding-down of the war in Afghanistan. As US forces were sent to the Philippines to challenge criminal gang Abu Sayyaf (alluded to as an Islamic terror group with ties to al-Qaeda), new facilities were constructed at RAF Edinburgh in Australia, and in Singapore and other island locales, to improve technical intelligence on the Philippines archipelago. Yemen, long mistrusted by the US because of its Marxist roots, despite the eventual reconciliation and merger of North and South Yemen, was asked to prove itself by helping to establish CIA facilities and private intelligence bases along its southern and eastern coasts.

To prepare for a new year without an ABM Treaty, Bush approved on January 2, 2002, the evolution of the Ballistic Missile Defense Organization into the Missile Defense Agency. The MDA could use vast classification authority, along with selective withholding of unclassified information, to prevent missile-defense details from being provided to the public in the post-September 11 environment. Defense Secretary Donald Rumsfeld gave the agency highly unusual exemptions from typical Pentagon procedures. The MDA did not have to follow rules that mandated military commanders to give exact military specifications for new weapons. It also did not have to report on a regular basis on its timelines and costs. In early 2003, additional special circumstances were suggested that would allow the MDA to field many weapon systems virtually without testing them.

Between the February 2002 military SpaceComm conference and the April 2002 National Space Symposium, NRO Director Peter Teets gave journalists unusually detailed looks at where national-security space missions were headed. Teets' byword in early 2002 was 'persistence,' and how the notion of total situational awareness meant more than just total regional coverage, but continuous intelligence coverage of all areas over long periods of time. He hinted that this would entail both more space-based intelligence platforms, and better in-space inter-satellite links to make sure that all satellite systems provided a synchronized intelligence product. The later approval of a Transformational Communications Office that included NASA, underscored the decision that NASA and commercial satellites would play a critical role in the 'persistent' NRO product from now on.

Like 'transformation,' the word 'persistence' could mean many things to many people. Adm. James Ellis, commander of the US Strategic Command, told the 2003 Space Symposium that 'persistence can come from a geosynchronous SIGINT satellite, or from a Rivet Joint plane, or from Special Operations forces, or from an unmanned sensor platform on a battlefield. The challenge for us is to find the right balance.'

Teets always was frank in saying that the SBIRS-High, GPS-III, and Future Imagery Architecture satellite systems all were well above budget and behind schedule, with SBIRS-High in particular invoking some automatic governmental review as mandated by Congress. A software suite called SBIRS-High Increment 1, which could meld information from SBIRS-High and DSP, had been successfully installed at Buckley Field by the end of 2002 – several quarters late, to be sure, though researchers said its ability to filter different types of infrared targets, as well as its ability to screen out electromagnetic interference effects, had been improved significantly due to the delay. The satellites under development by Lockheed-Martin and its subcontractors, however, had run into multiple problems, including bad glues that made the telescope structure of SBIRS-High separate from the flexors holding the system in place. By the time the MDA awarded the SBIRS-Low contract to TRW (later acquired by Northrop-Grumman) in August 2002, the name of the low-earth program had been changed to Space Tracking and Surveillance System, perhaps in part to overcome the bad luck associated with the SBIRS acronym. Air Force Secretary James Roche said in early 2003 that he was 'trying to get out from under the SBIRS-High mess, and we are committed to not letting it happen again.'

The NRO did not consider the SBIRS-High/STSS combination enough to support wars through active tracking of moving targets. Teets constantly reiterated the need for a Space-Based Radar in order to spot moving targets on the ground. Congress had remained cold to the NRO's earlier proposal for a Discoverer II radar satellite that would combine talents of the NRO and NASA, but Teets was not about to give up on a new radar network that would augment the capabilities of Lacrosse/Onyx. He told a dinner audience in April 2003 that the Space-Based Radar could be as useful, if not more so, for tactical ground forces as it is for national command authorities, saying SBR 'will act as the forward eyes for strike platforms,' pointing out in particular the value of terrain-mapping for Special Operations forces.[1]

The Evolved Expendable Launch Vehicle had run into problems in both the Boeing Delta-IV launcher program, with a questionable RL-10 rocket engine, and with the Lockheed-Martin Atlas V program, based on a Russian-produced engine, the RD-180. There had been hints at the February 2002 meeting that the NRO would standardize on one EELV or another, yet Boeing and Lockheed-Martin received funding in early 2003 to insure continuation of both rocket architectures. Still, Teets called for continuing research in both a truly Reusable Launch Vehicle, or RLV, as well as the military space plane, a favored project of the Air Force with a requirement of placing at least 15,000 pounds in low-earth orbit (NASA was demanding a 45,000-pound capability for any joint space–plane project).

The involvement of Boeing in the EELV program, however, came to a sudden and inglorious end in July 2003. On July 24, Teets announced that $1.3 billion in EELV contracts for the Delta-IV would be given to Lockheed and its Atlas V, and that three Boeing business units would be barred from bidding on government launch contracts because of contract improprieties. Allegations had circulated for months that Boeing had hired a

Lockheed engineer to work for them, based on his access to details of the Atlas V program. While Boeing had admitted to having improper access to some Lockheed documents through the period of 1999 to 2002, Teets said in the summer of 2003 that evidence indicated that Boeing had more than 25,000 pages of Lockheed documents on the EELV internally. Teets said that Boeing had committed 'serious and substantial violations of federal law,' and added it was the biggest incident of corporate crime he had ever seen. No media representatives at the July press conference asked about Teets' former association with Lockheed, and whether he was impartial as NRO director in ruling on the EELV matter.

The decision was a critical blow to Boeing, however. A week earlier, the company announced it was dropping out of commercial space business. Its commercial aircraft business was in such jeopardy that Boeing considered eliminating the 757 airliner. After the EELV decision, Boeing also talked of canceling the Delta-IV. The only business Boeing still could rely on was its two large spy satellite contracts with the NRO, which were unaffected by the EELV decision. The NRO turned its West Coast launches over to Lockheed, who had sole responsibility for EELV spy satellite flights from Vandenberg Air Force Base, flights which would include sensitive special-purpose polar-orbit launches.

Teets was still living under the budget restrictions enacted in response to NRO accountability problems in early 1996. He complained that, even though there were twelve national-security space launches scheduled for 2003, there had been only one in 2002, and programs like Future Imagery Architecture and Intruder appeared far behind their initial development timelines. The NRO was particularly dependent upon a single prime contractor, Boeing, responsible for both FIA and Intruder. The former program was large enough that it was cited by some financial analysts as being the sole factor that kept the Orange County area, where Boeing retained most of its FIA-related workforce, from sliding into recession in 2001. But the tiny amount of information coming out on FIA and Intruder in 2002 did not give the NRO faith that Boeing could meet mid-decade commitments.[2]

In response, Rumsfeld met with CIA Director George Tenet in early December 2002, to talk about 'reprogramming' between

$625 million and $900 million in intelligence funding to attempt to get spy-satellite programs back on track. While some Washington analysts claimed that FIA was facing problems because of the massive size of each satellite, the planned constellation of a dozen FIA satellites actually would use smaller individual satellites than many signals intelligence or KH series satellites. Boeing's $4 billion FIA program faced delays more for its complexity – by attempting to design complex analytical and relay systems that could handle both close-look and broad mapping tasks, Boeing and the intelligence community at large had bumped against the limits of what was possible.

While the Air Force and the NRO had not chosen a deputy for military space in early 2002, Teets announced that Air Force Maj. Gen. Mike Hamel would be in charge of a Directorate of National Security Space Integration. Brig. Gen. Steve Ferrell was chosen as the new National Security Space Architect, while Lt. Gen. Brian Arnold was named Program Executive Officer for Space.

Teets was unusually candid with the House Armed Services Committee in March 2003, when he discussed the NRO and Air Force 'offensive counter-space,' or OCS operations. These include the Counter Communication System, in which an adversary's military satellite operations can be disrupted, slated for initial testing in fiscal 2004; and Counter Surveillance Reconnaissance System, which disrupts an adversary's use of satellite imagery. In his analysis of the hearing, Steve Aftergood of the Federation of American Scientists revealed that Teets said that the NRO wants 'the ability to see everything and know everything, while simultaneously denying our adversaries both the ability to do the same, and the knowledge that such capabilities are being used against them.'[3] During his March 12 testimony, Teets was very explicit in pointing out that the same systems are used for missile defense, intelligence collection, and war-fighting. He used SBIRS-High as an example of how the NRO sees multiple missions, pointing out that the infrared sensors on the SBIRS-High satellites are used for both intelligence and theater ballistic missile warning. On that same day, Maj. Gen. Judd Blaisdell, director of Air Force space operations, said that 'we are so dominant in space that I pity a country that would come up against us.'

A new space role not widely appreciated when announced was the UAV management duties of Director of Defense Research and

Engineering Ron Sega, who was tasked with defining a new National Aerospace Initiative, uniting development plans for UAVs, micro-satellites, and other autonomous vehicles that spanned air and space. While the NAI primarily looks at new propulsion concepts such as ramjets and scramjets, with a goal of evolving cheap rocket propulsion so that Mach number equals year ('Mach 7 by 2007!'), Sega also is examining common infrastructure for satellites and UAVs. He also heads up a DARPA 'Surveillance and Knowledge Systems' study, applying the same cross-border thinking to the use of intelligence.

The success of the Predator and Global Hawk in Afghanistan encouraged all the services to accelerate their programs for autonomous vehicles in war. The Defense Department's Tactical Mobile Robots Program, of joint interest to Army, Marines, and Air Force, began testing next-generation devices that could improve upon the performance of ground robots used in the assault on the caves of Tora Bora. Vehicles like the M-Bot from Science Applications International Corp., Spike from Charles Draper Labs and the PackBot from iRobot Inc., could use a combination of GPS navigational tools and 'WiFi' 802.11 wireless local area networks to operate as a team, using 'swarm intelligence' or 'hive behavior' to conduct coordinated surveillance and assault on remote and/or dangerous targets. Similarly, the Navy's Space and Naval Warfare Systems Center began tests in the summer of 2002, on behalf of Navy Seals, on using Autonomous Underwater Vehicles, or AUVs, for mine-detection and anti-submarine warfare. One spinoff of the Woods Hole Oceanographic Institute, Hydroid Inc., has developed naval AUVs optimized for warfare, including the Remus, a 5-foot-long shallow-water sub. A more advanced combat drone, the Manta, is being designed to spread acoustic buoys and alert a 'mothership' for warfare.

Sega has emphasized in the new NAI program that the Air Force needs to stop making false distinctions between UAVs, micro-satellites, low-earth orbit satellite swarms, and similar vehicles that could act in complementary fashion, as a unified military unit for combat or surveillance. General Dynamics was a particular fan of this 'swarm' concept, promoting the idea of distributing both control-intelligence and interception tasks across a cluster of large UAVs, beginning with Boeing's X-45

UCAV. The eventual goal was to apply the lessons learned to swarms of very small UAVs, ranging in size from a model plane to a dragonfly, in which the distributed smarts of the robotic swarm would show unique 'emergent' intelligence not anticipated by the designers of the UAVs. The implication of emergent behavior may have been frightening to those steeped in peaceful uses of robotics, though it did not seem to concern DARPA.[4]

By the summer of 2002, the Global Hawk's use in imaging intelligence was being expanded in a Northrop Grumman project with EADS Systems and Defence Electronics, in order to provide Global Hawk with an electronic intelligence package for standoff listening duties. In a Defense Department technology wish-list document from 1999, DARPA officials already were waxing about the same types of persistent, global total situational awareness, accomplished through intelligent swarms of UAVs and satellites, that Teets longed for in his February 2002 speech. To help achieve 'persistence,' the US Air Force Research Laboratory is even considering nuclear-powered UAVs that could loiter over battle areas for months at a time. In February 2003, *New Scientist* magazine described feasibility studies, run from the lab at Kirtland Air Force Base in New Mexico, to plan a nuclear-powered version of Global Hawk.

One obvious problem, ignored by UAV proponents, is the lack of operational responsibility and possible civil liberties infractions involved in putting fire-and-forget, death-at-a-distance responsibilities in the purview of robots. This is not simply a worry for Iraq and beyond. On November 3, 2002, a CIA Predator launched from Djibouti fired Hellfire missiles at a car in Yemen with six suspected al-Qaeda members. All six died, including a US citizen. The Defense Department was sure of their al-Qaeda role, and thus classified them as 'enemy combatants,' not subject to human rights. But if the November event could take place with few complaints from the human rights community, how often will we put the power of life and death, in large-scale war or in small-scale assaults on terror, under the control of robots?

In preparation for withdrawal from the ABM Treaty in June 2002, the Defense Department took important steps in reorienting space missions, ones that were not widely recognized at the time, but which would prove important in establishing permanent war on rogue states. In regard to the interceptor warheads for the ground-based programs planned for Alaska, Rumsfeld proposed in April 2002 that the MDA consider nuclear-tipped rockets, a concept that had been rejected long ago in the Safeguard-Sentinel system design (Congress later in 2003 placed a specific ban on such a program). Going nuclear obviously allowed each interceptor to be less accurate, and more able to overcome countermeasures, but the Rumsfeld proposal bore another relation to the planned merger of Space Command and Strategic Command, involving how nuclear and conventional weapons are considered as unified battle tools.

That merger was part of a shell game that involved the creation of a new domestic unified command for homeland defense, the Northern Command, which US Space Command commander Ed Eberhart was chosen to lead in late April 2002. By situating Northern Command at the US Space Command headquarters at Peterson Air Force Base in Colorado Springs, the Air Force allowed continued oversight of NORAD missions at nearby Cheyenne Mountain Air Force Station, the aging missile-monitoring base deep inside Cheyenne Mountain. In fact, NORAD was supposed to fall under Northern Command, though the Air Force could not quite specify how the Canadian government would feel about suddenly being frozen out of effective control of homeland defense for the North American continent.

There was a more chilling aspect to the formation of Northern Command. Eberhart had intimate familiarity with many of the tools developed by the NRO and DARPA for space-based monitoring, analysis, and coordination of intelligence for war-fighting. This toolbox could be applied to any duty deemed appropriate for homeland defense, and by extension, could be provided to the civilian Department of Homeland Security (DHS). Northern Command officials insisted throughout the summer and fall of 2002 that they were acutely aware of civil liberties issues, but the commonality of contractor duties showed how easy the 'technological creep' from space control would be. Even prior to the DHS' formation, key space contractors were involved in Immigration and Naturalization Service body- and iris-scan programs for border searches, and in Transportation Security Agency monitoring tools. Raytheon provided a particu-larly interesting example of multiple-use functions: its intelligence-processing outsourcing facility across the street from

Buckley Field in Aurora, Colorado, while serving the NSA and the NRO for post-downlink processing, also served as a secure Web hosting site, and as a ground station for the upcoming N-POESS satellite jointly sponsored by NASA, the NRO, and the NOAA. Eberhart did little to quell fears of homeland misuse of space tools, when he hosted a series of meetings with government agencies and contractors prior to the attack on Iraq, explaining how homeland-monitoring duties would be carried out during wartime. In his April 2003 speech before the National Space Symposium, Eberhart said that 'situational awareness' for Northern Command meant that his command should, as early as possible, share intelligence with state and local law-enforcement agencies promptly. Over the longer term, intelligence from these multiple sources could be integrated, 'and ideally, fused into a seamless whole along with open-source information.'

This normalization of monitoring functions within Northern Command made the year-end 2002 tempest involving John Poindexter's Total Information Awareness program in DARPA seem a little silly. The tools Poindexter wanted to use, involving the data-mining and database analysis tools developed by everyone, from familiar CIA and NSA hands like Oracle Corp. to newcomers like Groove Networks and ChoicePoint Inc., were direct descendants of the keyword programs used by NSA in Echelon, as well as the data-mining tools used by private corporations in 'one-to-one marketing' schemes. What Poindexter wanted to do for DARPA's benefit was something that already had been internalized by the NRO, the NSA, and Space Command, and that was being adopted by Northern Command through its contractors' programs.

To cite but a single example of the type of tools prime contractors were applying in the civilian monitoring realm, Northrop-Grumman had developed a 'WebTAS,' or Web-enabled Timeline Analysis System, in conjunction with Air Force Research Labs, which had been installed at the Prince Sultan Air Base in Saudi Arabia as the Master Attack Air Planning tool for Operation Iraqi Freedom. The software could call up maps of specific areas, and clicking on highlighted links from within the maps could reference multiple SIGINT, RADINT, or other specific databases to provide information on the person or vehicle highlighted. It could also apply a behavioral filter to allow the software itself to identify targets of concern, providing patterns of behavior which the intelligence planner could decide to act upon. In the spring of 2003, Northrop-Grumman was pursuing civilian accounts for WebTAS both within Northern Command, and independently with local law enforcement agencies and regional counter-drug alliances. Even as John Poindexter's Information Awareness Office at the Pentagon was being hindered by a Congress rightfully frightened of civil liberties implications, contractors working with Space Command and Northern Command were offering tools more sophisticated than any Poindexter talked about.

Domestic agencies also appeared, at the end of 2002, to be bidding their way into Sega's aerospace program for more effective use of UAVs. Both the Coast Guard and Border Patrol units of the Department of Homeland Security, as well as the Transportation and Energy Departments, were clamoring for the use of UAVs for a variety of homeland security tasks. The FBI specifically wanted to use UAVs to augment an existing airborne reconnaissance program called 'Nightstalker,' using propeller planes and helicopters to track targets of interest.

The new total monitoring environment for North America must be seen in the context of other agencies' loosened restrictions. Lt. Gen. Michael Hayden, director of the National Security Agency, suggested in Congress in mid-October 2002 that it was time for the NSA to resume domestic monitoring of potential threats within the US, removing specific restrictions enacted in the mid-1970s. Meanwhile, John Ashcroft was playing a tough line with the Foreign Intelligence Surveillance Act. In August 2002, the Foreign Intelligence Surveillance Court, the nation's secret 'star chambers' court for approving foreign-interest wiretaps, claimed that the Justice Department was abusing the USA Patriot Act by allowing prosecutors to misuse intelligence information. Ashcroft called for the first meeting in history of the FISC's Appeals Court, which ruled in early 2003 that the Justice Department's methods were appropriate. Soon after the war on Iraq began, the US Supreme Court refused to hear challenges to the USA Patriot's intelligence provisions, in effect handing Ashcroft the blank check for domestic surveillance he sought.

Another important factor often was ignored in the so-called death of US Space Command, and its transfer to Strategic

Command at Offut Air Force Base, Nebraska. The Air Force Space Command was being simultaneously elevated in importance, through the assignment of its first four-star general, Gen. Lance Lord, to a position overseeing AFSC. By making the Air Force the primary executive agent for space within the Defense Department, naming Teets the primary procurement officer for space, and giving Lord the commanding role at AFSC, Rumsfeld was keeping the Space Command infrastructure relatively intact.

At the same time, however, the national Space Command layer was merged with Strategic Command for a good reason, according to the Rumsfeld view of the world. US Space Command already had won control over nuclear missiles. It had become the primary agency for conducting federal government computer-network defense, and computer-network assault. By putting these elements within Strategic Command, the Defense Department was affirming that space had become a fully normal element of US strategic control. Further, nuclear weapons were now considered a necessary element of the suite of control tools. The firebreak between conventional weapons and nuclear weapons now was disappearing, in an era where deterrence was deemed irrelevant.

Conservative analysts enamored with the 'revolution in military affairs' (RMA) were puzzled by this Space Command merger with Strategic Command, because many favored RMA precisely because it depended on conventional precision weapons. To the analysis group STRATFOR, for example, Rumsfeld was tying US Space Command to a nuclear dinosaur. But the defense secretary knew exactly what he was doing. The Bush administration believed in RMA, but without any support of deterrence, RMA had to include the use of nuclear weapons by default. This was codified on September 14, 2002, with the signing of National Security Presidential Directive 17, which spelled out that the US 'reserves the right to respond with over-whelming force – including potentially nuclear weapons – to the use of weapons of mass destruction against the United States, our forces abroad, and friends and allies.' What this meant in practice was indicated when Gen. Lord told the 2003 Space Symposium what he meant by the transition of strategic nuclear weapons. Air Force Space Command was planning force modernization in conjunction with Strategic Command, which could involve returning to the old concept of mobile missiles (similar to the MX) under a new program called Minuteman-IV, and considering the combined placement of ICBMs bearing nuclear and conventional weapons within one missile field. Both mobile missiles and conventionally-armed ICBMs would break existing treaty constraints, but the Bush administration had not shown, with ABM or other treaties, much concern over preserving the existing treaty infrastructure.[5]

A final telling factor in this transition was announced in late April 2002, just prior to the administration crystallizing its ABM Treaty withdrawal. The Air Force eliminated its deputy chief of staff for communications and information, and replaced it with a deputy chief of staff for warfighting integration. For the Air Force, all 'C4ISR' (Command, Control, Communications, Computers, Intelligence, Surveillance, Reconnaissance) functions now served in fighting and winning permanent war, and should be recognized and identified as such.

The timing of these actions was by no means accidental. George Bush officially committed the nation to a doctrine of pre-emptive warfare against any state of the US's choosing in a speech to West Point Military Academy on June 1, 2002. Given the planning that had gone into attacking Iraq in the first half of 2002, many analysts treated the conclusions of the speech, advocating first-strike attack whenever a potential threat of weapons of mass destruction was discerned, as a foregone conclusion. In briefings to the president in late June, Rumsfeld and Joint Chiefs Chairman Richard Myers said that the merger of US Space Command and Strategic Command was to allow the creation of a unified command capable of carrying out such pre-emptive warfare, and integration of strategic nuclear missiles with ballistic missile defense.

Bush timed the official consummation of ABM Treaty withdrawal well, approving construction to begin June 15, 2002 on the Ground-based Midcourse Defense Test Bed at Fort Greely, Alaska. Something odd was happening to the plans for X-band radars in Alaska, however. While campaigns for Fylingdales and Thule upgrades continued apace, the Missile Defense Agency began letting contracts in early August for a sea-based X-band radar, constructed on a platform resembling an oil rig, which would be used in a traveling sea-based test bed to support Alaska and Kwajalein tests. While the sea-based X-band radar was scarcely out of its conceptual stages at this point, it had already come under fiscal scrutiny by late 2003. Independent intelligence analyst Allen Thomson wrote to Rep. Solomon Ortiz of Texas in July 2003, suggesting that there were improprieties in the use of tax funds in acquiring 'Moss Sirius,' the sea-based platform used for the X-band radar. Thomson said that as much as $200 million in Missile Defense Agency funds could have been misused in the acquisition and conversion of the Moss Sirius platform, and suggested that the entire sea-based X-band radar program might have to be scrutinized carefully by MDA critics.[6]

No Nukes North, an Alaska anti-Star Wars group, staged a peace camp at Fort Greely during the latter half of June, but faced a population split between basic sympathy for arguments against missile defense, and those who felt the new ground-based system would 'protect' Alaska. The details of how and where the modified Scud-B target missiles would be launched, and of the type of missions that would take place at Kodiak Launch Center on Kodiak Island on Alaska's southern coast, were classified as secret by the MDA. The agency also insisted on classifying all detailed cost breakdowns for production and deployment schedules of the interceptor missiles. Philip Coyle III, an assistant secretary of defense in the Clinton administration who always insisted on adequate testing, speculated in June 2002 that these details were being classified to prevent the public from learning how much the target missiles failed to represent actual warheads a BMD weapon might encounter, and hence how many tests would be necessary to provide a minimal level of assurance that the weapons worked. The information was not just being kept from the public and from Congress; it was even being kept from Defense Department groups like the Office of Operational Test and Evaluation.

During the summer, testing of short-range Navy missile defense continued apace, despite the cancellation of the Area Missile Defense program. On June 13, a Navy SM-3 missile fired from the USS *Lake Erie* cruiser in the Pacific shot down an Aries dummy missile fired from the Pacific Missile Range in Kauai, Hawaii. Again, Coyle criticized the Navy program as proving nothing about the ability to distinguish real warheads from decoys. An Aegis cruiser, however, proved essential in allowing a successful test of an interceptor launched from Kwajalein on October 15, 2002 – because the ABM Treaty no longer controlled use of secondary sea-based radar, the Aegis cruiser was able to use its SPY-1 radar to provide important radar information to the interceptor.

In July 2002, Defense Department officials began touring European countries in a rerun of the missile-defense promotional tours in the spring of 2001 – except this time, the administration had the club of an abandoned ABM Treaty and construction starts in Alaska with which to bludgeon reluctant allies. The public meeting had been preceded by a secret conference in Colorado Springs in April 2002 between Lt. Gen. Ron Kadish and Brig. Gen. Trey Obering of MDA, and representatives from five NATO nations, who discussed the advantages their countries might receive as partners within a global MDA plan. Turkey was pressured into accepting a new early-warning radar, Britain was asked to provide new radar technology and use of its Type 45 destoyers in missile-defense applications, and several nations were asked to consider ground-based interceptors.

The only program to suffer in the new MDA program was the Space-Based Laser (SBL). In a preview of the eventual fall closure of the SBL Program Office, Senate and House negotiators shifted $30 million in late June from the SBL program to the Airborne Laser. The ABL had problems of its own. With a mission of shooting down intermediate systems only, the Boeing 747 plane already was 5,000 pounds above its maximum weight of 175,000 pounds, but an order by MDA to expand the ABL by allowing it to shoot down intercontinental missiles as well, promised to make the weight problem far worse. *Defense News* claimed in March 2003 that the ABL was running into a fundamental clash between missions and capabilities. Nevertheless, the ABL appeared to be so far ahead of the SBL, in both concept and implementation, that Congressional leaders agreed with the Defense Department that space-based weapons be put on the back burner. In an October 31, 2002, briefing with reporters, MDA head Lt. Gen. Ronald Kadish said that the initial 2012 tests for SBL had been canceled, no test facilities would be built, and 'we will do technology as aggressively as we can, but it won't be focused on putting an experiment in space in the near term.'

That was not the case with the ground-based interceptor program, however. As part of an effort to sway Blair's Defence

Secretary Geoff Hoon, Lt. Gen. Kadish came to Fylingdales in October and insisted that the entire US missile-defense infra-structure would be up and running in five years, and that it was time for Britain to get on board. This was followed up by a formal request in mid-December to the British government for Fyling-dales' use, along with a similar request to the Danish government for a Thule upgrade in Greenland, a speed which the British American Security Information Council characterized as 'indecent haste.'

The reason for a hasty announcement became obvious when the first phase of missile defense was officially announced in December in Washington. On December 17, President Bush signed National Security Presidential Directive 23, calling for initial operating capability for a ground-based system to be fielded in 2004–05. Ironically, only six days earlier an exoat-mospheric kill vehicle test conducted from Vandenberg and Kwajalein had failed, due to a single integrated circuit on the kill vehicle that failed to tell the vehicle to separate from its booster rocket. As Defense Department officials had told MDA officers, though, the viability of the weapons used in the first-generation system were not an issue that concerned Bush.

The initial intent to put full X-band radar capability in Shemya, Clear, Fylingdales, and Thule suddenly had disappeared in the president's December order, with the transportable X-band test bed being the only remaining radar in that frequency band. Because the Air Force was not convinced that the X-band system was ready, the military was revamping the existing Cobra Dane intelligence radar on Shemya to handle warhead tracking calcu-lations. And what the British and Danish governments were being asked to do was to upgrade existing UHF facilities, as well as computers that could track warheads faster. Since the announcement was being made at the beginning of the US and European Christmas recess, few reporters were around to ask about the X-band shell game. The interceptor rockets, too, were facing severe problems due to the use of unreliable modified Minuteman missiles as boosters, and few questions were asked about what would be done to the boosters to insure a fielded system by late 2004. Besides, military-affairs reporters had bigger fish to fry: the US was going to war.

George Bush's meetings with advisors at his Crawford, Texas ranch in the third week of August are often cited as the point at which an attack on Iraq was firmly decided. The White House claimed at the time that the meeting was primarily about missile defense. Both interpretations were correct. Bush and his aides were discussing the ways in which space-based military programs and multi-tiered missile defense would allow first-strike attack to be conducted against nations the US judged were too close to acquiring weapons of mass destruction.

In many senses, an attack on Iraq was inevitable long before late August. And it is certainly a correct interpretation to say that the presentations of September and October before the UN Security Council were simply a fig leaf, designed to give an aura of respectability to a decision already made. The only thing different between September 2002 and March 2003 in the UN Security Council is that the majority of permanent members were willing to be bamboozled once, for the sake of appeasing the US, but were not willing to be bamboozled a second time.

The new opposition was enabled in part by Gerhard Schroder using a peace platform as a means of winning his 2002 re-election as prime minister. The German government took careful note of a speech Vice President Richard Cheney made to a veterans' group in late August 2002, which virtually committed the United States to an attack on Iraq. French President Jacques Chirac, nominally seen as the most conservative and pro-US politician within the current French landscape, recognized the legitimacy of the complaints regarding US behavior made by members of Lionel Jospin's government, and began heavily criticizing US buildup by the end of 2002, even as UN arms inspectors returned to Iraq.

While some buildup at Diego Garcia and Prince Sultan Air Base could have been conducted in secret, the Bush administration showed little desire to hide its plans during the weeks in which arms inspectors briefly returned to Iraq. The al-Udeid base in Qatar was established as a central 'fan-out' logistics base from which more 'virtual,' FOL-like bases could be created. As numbers of troops on the ground and on aircraft carriers in the Persian Gulf exceeded 100,000 and then 200,000, al-Udeid sported new airfields and new satellite dishes established by the 50th Space Wing of the Air Force Space Command. By the time the

Combined Air Operations Center was up and running at Prince Sultan in early March, hundreds of representatives of the 50th Space Wing were there. Portable space dishes and smaller UAV fields were created in very public places – the entire northern half of Kuwait, for example, became a massive American base centered on the 'Camps of the States': Camp New York, Camp New Jersey, etc. Existing naval bases like the Bahrain Sixth Fleet facility were expanded. Meanwhile, however, intelligence and space-control bases were upgraded in a more quiet fashion, particularly in multiple locations in Oman. Russian sources claimed that, despite Jordan's official declaration of neutrality, several hundred US special ops and signals intelligence troops were sent to the Zarka military base in the new year.

Since DARPA was well aware that the NRO was having a tough time finding funding for the Space-Based Radar, and that no radar capable of finding moving targets from space would be in place for the launch of the war on Iraq, the agency began tests before the war on Afghanistan with what it called Affordable Moving Surface Target Engagement (AMSTE). Using the Joint STARS plane that proved itself in the Gulf War, DARPA coordinated its information with an array of Ground Moving-Target Indicator radars, fusing the information together to allow the continuous tracking of moving targets. The information then could be sent to a dumb or smart weapon, including GPS-guided bombs like JDAM, and UCAV robot planes armed with missiles. The similarities with the Talon programs for intelligence were not accidental. While the program never moved beyond the test phase during the Afghan War, by late 2001 the AMSTE program proved capable of fusing information from Joint STARS, a U-2 with Synthetic Aperture Radar, a Global Hawk, and a BAC-11 aircraft simulating a Joint Strike Fighter radar system. Northrop Grumman won two phases of contracts in 2002 and 2003 to extend the integration of search radars with JDAM bombs and Joint Standoff Weapons. Some of these test systems were reportedly sent to Qatar in February 2003, though their use in the Iraq assault has not been confirmed.

An important point that virtually assured UN Security Council breakdown was hit when the Turkish parliament denied the pre-positioning of US forces in that nation on March 1. A more patient administration would have interpreted intransigence from Turkey, a loyal American ally of fifty years' standing, as an indication that more cautious diplomacy was needed to launch the war. Instead, plans were immediately shifted to emphasize southern fronts and carrier-borne troop landings, and Turkey's refusal seemed to serve only to harden the resolve of George Bush and Tony Blair.

In public, the rift between the US and British 'Atlantic Bridge' alliance on the one hand, and the remaining members of the Security Council on the other, constituted the most significant breakdown in alliance relations since the end of World War II. Due more to US brashness than French intransigence, the US government created the conditions in early March 2003 for the possible dissolution of NATO, NORAD, and the UKUSA pact, as well as the permanent souring of Security Council relations. Yet, despite the protestations of Secretary of State Colin Powell and UN Ambassador John Negroponte, neither Bush nor Blair put much care into preserving Security Council relations for the sake of losing a few weeks in initiating the war. If they did, various Canadian and French compromise proposals for expanding the arms-inspection programs could have been discussed, debated, and discussed again. The British effort to reach a partial compromise could have been promoted through the second half of March 2003, rather than being dropped rather abruptly on March 14. The reason diplomacy came to naught was scarcely due to European fears or insistence on no invasion. It was solely due to George Bush's desire to launch a war by mid-March, with or without UN Security Council support.

Given the loose chatter about 'shock and awe' that was promoted from the Wolfowitz wing in early 2003, the F-117 air attacks early in the morning of March 20 appeared to be an anti-climactic way to begin a major war. Part of the reason for the subtle and abrupt end to the 48-hour 'ultimatum' given to Hussein was the desire to take advantage of immediate intelligence on a meeting of the Iraqi leadership, which held out the promise of 'decapitating' the Ba'ath Party. But part may also have been due, oddly enough, to a massive blizzard that hit the Rocky Mountains March 17–18, completely closing down the critical space bases of Cheyenne Mountain, Buckley, Peterson, and Schriever for the first time in history. Defense Department officials refused to comment on the impact the closures had on the war, but an odd 36-hour lull followed the initial cruise missile attacks. While troops moved in formations to the Kuwait–Iraq border, coordinated air campaigns did not begin until March 22. But as soon as Schriever reopened in late March, the base's Space Warfare Center initiated its second-generation space warfare test, Schriever II, though officials insisted it had nothing to do with the extant war.

In two separate efforts to decapitate the Iraqi leadership, military leaders took pride in saying that attack planning from the Combined Air Operations Center (CAOC) took only minutes or a couple of hours. The March 20 strike, on an underground bunker using EGBU-27 bombs, was targeted based on a mix of signals intelligence, and airborne UAV intelligence from Predators regularly flying over Baghdad in mid-March. An April 8 assault on what was believed to be Saddam's hideout in Baghdad had a lag time of only 45 minutes between initial signals and human intelligence reports, and B-1 assaults using JDAM bombs.

Air Force Secretary James Roche reminded the 2003 National Space Symposium of two important factors during those assaults: first, US and British forces had spent nine months, between July 2002 and the start of the war, decimating the Iraqi Air Force infrastructure, with the result that not a single plane or missile was launched before US troops entered Baghdad, which Roche called 'air and space domination to the max.' Second, the very dominance with which UAVs could provide intelligence throughout Iraq was due to their space-based control and coordination. Roche said that without space dominance, there would be no Predators or Global Hawks.

This dominance included a star role for GPS. Gen. Lord said that more than 60 percent of all aerial bombardment was undertaken using GPS bombs. Although the Iraqis tried to use GPS jammers as electronic countermeasures during the early days of the war, the jammers were destroyed using GPS-guided JDAM bombs.

'GPS puts the DAM in JDAM,' Lord said. Thomas Moorman, a former head of Space Command now with Booz Allen Hamilton Inc., said that he utterly rejected the notion that Operation Iraqi Freedom was less a space war than Desert Storm or Enduring Freedom. In reality, the use of space was an order of magnitude greater in the Iraq attack, he said, and the only reason 'embedded' reporters failed to realize this was because they were traveling with ground troops, and because the use of space had become so normalized.

NASA had a role to play in the slow move from Basra to Baghdad, this time filling in for data that the Defense Meteorological Satellite Program (DMSP) weather satellites couldn't provide. A radiometer called MODIS aboard NASA Aqua and Terra satellites provided better information about the dust storms encountered along the Euphrates River from March 23 to March 26, than any Pentagon or NRO satellite could provide. Officials with the joint-agency National Polar-Orbit Operational Environmental Satellite System (N-POESS) said that one factor driving joint weather work by NIMA, NRO, NASA, and DoD was that new weather instruments could be tested and fielded on N-POESS satellites, allowing better response to using weather prediction for war-fighting, than typically seen in Defense Department weather satellites.

NIMA and the NRO made critical use of commercial satellite imagery in the government's ClearView program, committing to buy up to $500 million of images from Space Imaging and DigitalGlobe to fill in gaps from the NRO's own satellite. As the war progressed, NIMA promised to follow up with a NextView program, entailing $100 million worth of funding to commercial imaging companies a year, though the federal government would expect a say in aiding the design of the companies' next-generation satellites.[7]

Like Afghanistan, the number of Iraqi dead, believed to be under 2,000 in mid-April, was far less than what might have occurred if 'shock and awe' had lived up to its advance billing. But the Rumsfeld–Wolfowitz rulebook for 'smart war' only appears partially humane when stacked against the Powell doctrine of overwhelming force utilized in Desert Storm. If massive air bombardment, using smart and dumb bombs alike, had been employed from March 20 on, an occupation of Baghdad might have been possible within days, albeit at a very high cost of civilian life in Iraq. If a positive element can be seen in the Rumsfeld battle strategy, it lies in the defense secretary's recognition that civilian casualties must always be kept to a minimum, a goal which often put Rumsfeld in contention with Central Command head Gen. Tommy Franks.

But the limitations of smart, high-tech war from space were evident within a week of the initial invasion. Intelligent decapitation only achieves astonishing success when the population at large is anxious to be liberated. Wolfowitz, in particular, had convinced many within the Defense Department that Iraqi civilians would be rushing to embrace the liberators within hours of the first troop crossings. The fact that a first-strike invasion force might be ardently opposed for nationalist reasons, even by citizens living under a dictator, never seems to have entered into the Wolfowitz equation. The result, as an April 2003 issue of *Business Week* pointed out, is that when high-tech elimination of critical infrastructure wreaks havoc on the leaders without winning the hearts and minds of the population, a war quickly reverts to the same kind of low-intensity, sapper- and terror-based conflict seen in Vietnam and Central America. As Maj. William Gillespie of the Army Third Infantry told *Business Week*, when Republican Guards are eliminated but the population is outraged, the weapons of choice turn to snipers in pickup trucks, suicide bombers, and booby-traps set up in scores of private homes throughout the nation. Many Iraqis were indeed glad to finally be rid of the entire Ba'ath regime by the time US troops entered Baghdad – yet European and Arab news sources pointed out that the scenes of Saddam statues being torn down in Baghdad took place in nearly-empty squares, seemingly stage-managed by Iraqis allied with US forces. The similarities to events like Guatemala in 1954 are obvious.

In some senses, the difficulty of warfare in Iraq taught the same kind of lessons on space-controlled unilateral planet-bossing that September 11 should have taught about ballistic missile defense. At some point, search-and-destroy missions must be limited to those fringe terrorists who legitimately practice catastrophism, while other nation-states and sub-nationalist groups must be confronted with some reformed type of deterrence. Weapons of mass destruction of many types have been let out of the bag, and are unlikely to be perfectly controlled by force alone. Therefore, an appropriate mix of official UN bodies, informal coalition efforts like the Missile Technology Control Regime, and clearly explicated deterrence philosophies must be used to challenge aggressors. September 11 did not prove the need for missile defense, because the low-tech methods employed by al-Qaeda activists showed that individual sacrificial acts of mass destruction always will prove easier to implement than building an intermediate or intercontinental missile. Similarly, high-tech methods of controlling recalcitrant states can often be foiled by low-level citizen efforts to avoid domination, if the citizens see the planetary controller as a conqueror rather than a liberator.

It is ironic but scarcely accidental that the bluster about controlling sea lanes or space lanes grows louder and more frantic as an empire meets the limits of its ability to control events. And the triumphalism displayed as US troops entered Baghdad in April was deafening. At the 2003 National Space Symposium, Lockheed-Martin displayed its new logo for electronic warfare equipment: 'We're not looking for a fair fight.' Col. Robert Kent Traylor, deputy director of space operations and integration for the Air Force, displayed a new patch used by the space operations group of the Air Force executive office: 'Air and Space Operations – The Superiority Complex.'

Col. Traylor and Brig. Gen. Obering of the MDA provided the Space Symposium with a preview of where missile defense could be headed next. Traylor said that the pre-attack air assaults on the Iraqi Air Force prove the value of using counter-air operations as a part of missile defense. If you can take out an adversary's entire air fields and missile fields in advance, he said, the accuracy of kill vehicles in space becomes less of a concern. 'The Air Force views active missile defense as a missed opportunity for counter-air operations,' Traylor said. 'A JDAM may be an easier way to take out a target than hitting a bullet with a bullet.'

For the ground-based tests in 2004, Brig. Gen. Obering said, expect to see highly flexible tests in which targets are launched from Vandenberg, Kodiak, or even from C-17 transport airplanes, while kill vehicles are launched from both Kwajalein and Vandenberg. Warheads will be tracked by Spy-1 radars on Aegis cruisers, by transportable X-band radars on oil derricks at sea, and by whatever radars have been put into action in Shemya, Clear, Fylingdales, and Thule.

Meanwhile, the NRO has massive new plans for satellite networks, part of the Transformational Communications Office launched in October 2002. Three 'transformational' satellite architectures already were in the pipeline: Advanced EHF was the next generation of Milstar, planned to include four cross-linked geosynchronous satellites offering ten times the data rate of Milstar. Wideband Gapfiller System, or WGS, was intended to follow up DSCS-2 and GBS capabilities with a dual-band, X-band and Ka-band service, providing 1.2-Gbits per second aggregate throughput. The steerable-beam system of WGS would provide reliable two-way service similar to GBS for the first time, and is slated to be launched beginning in 2004, from the EELV. Finally, narrowband voice services carried by GBS would be taken up by a new network of satellites and ground stations called MUOS, for Mobile User Objective System. MUOS is a Navy-managed system that would replace UHF Follow-On, with launches beginning in 2007.

But as Teets and Rear Adm. Rand Fisher described at the 2003 Space Symposium, the AEHF, WGS, and MUOS systems are only the beginning. The Transformational Communications Office inside the NRO has plans to make the space-dominance networks run by the NRO, DISA, and NASA the equivalent of a broadband Internet. The Transformational Communications Architecture would move from circuit to packet communications, and it would seek to relieve the most severe bottleneck, in the last mile to the user. Teets said in his April keynote speech that TCA will 'remove both bandwidth and access as constraints to the warfighter ... The effort is not about satellites, not about ground terminals, but about a whole new architecture to support our war-fighting efforts.'

Two additional satellite constellations would join AEHF, WGS, and MUOS under this plan. TSATs, or Transformational Satellites, will be protected Extremely High Frequency communication satellites operating in both Ka and X bands, with the possibility for communicating directly with MUOS. A second new satellite, the Advanced Polar Satellite, is a special high-speed satellite system handling IP and circuit-switched data, with an RF cross-link to the Advanced EHF satellite now under development. The Pentagon plans to spend at least $9.6 billion on TCA development, with $6.3 billion going to just the TSAT and APS satellites.

Former Space Command head Howell Estes said that when Defense Secretary Donald Rumsfeld opened the TCA Office in October 2002, the rationale for combining NRO and NASA resources was to 'close the last mile to the tactical war-fighter, by extending bandwidth to forces on the move.' Fisher, who serves as both program executive officer for MUOS and the director within the NRO for the TCA, said that a long wish-list exists for the TCA, with some services putting a high priority on nuclear survivability, while others want a dynamically adjustable communication system capable of supporting thin clients. Ideally, a single prime contractor would help coordinate these demands, Fisher said, but added that he doubted whether a single corporate contractor could juggle all the information necessary to satisfy NRO, Pentagon, and NASA demands.

Troy Meinke, deputy project leader in the Milsatcom Program Office at the Air Force Space and Missiles Center, said that planning already is under way for incorporating laser-based inter-satellite communications, as well as optical links to aircraft, into the overall TCA network. In fact, the Pentagon has programmed $260 million in the program for development of an Airborne Optical Satcom Terminal for the TCA.

If the Defense Department can develop effective network-management and provisioning software, the TCA network will be able to perform the same type of Quality of Service prioritiza-tion, even across agencies, that is performed in advanced Internet subnets. Ideally, Meinke said, two agencies could sign a Service Level Agreement for bandwidth in the same way two carriers or Internet Service Providers do today. Fisher said that the best aspect of the TCA program is the elimination of parallel and superfluous space programs across military and civilian agencies. 'If I can glue an architecture together with common standards and protocols, I care less about the specific organizations developing this,' Fisher said.[8]

In order to provide fast support for global battles, the Air Force Space Command is planning for a rapid-relaunch capability far different than NASA's Orbital Space Plane. In early March 2003, the Space Command unveiled its Operationally Responsive Spacelift plan, studying ways to reuse space vehicles, put satellites into orbit on short notice, and launch counter-space weapons. Since a true reuseable launch vehicle may be many years away, one of the drivers for using ICBMs for conventional munitions, mentioned earlier, is to provide the fastest possible way to move weapons into space. The ORS program also will work along with the DARPA National Aerospace Initiative to consider launching micro-satellites on F-15E fighters, or larger satellites on special cheap launchers that would augment the EELV.[9]

In July 2003, DARPA disclosed details of one of the first such space vehicles to support ORS, a hypersonic cruise drone to be developed under the program FALCON (Force Application and Launch from Continental US). DARPA envisions a drone that could carry loads of up to 12,000 pounds, capable of being launched from a conventional runway, which could hit any spot within 9,000 miles in less than two hours, dropping bombs, sensors, or autonomous vehicles in any region without the need for a forward military base. While many assaults on Iraq in 2003 were carried out by planes launched from Missouri on one-day bombing missions, the FALCON drone would allow immediate strike capability from the high stratosphere or low space, using only US bases as a platform for global war.

Since NASA has been playing a key support role in providing information for military campaigns, it is important to conclude with a mention of how tightly integrated the civilian agency is with its Pentagon allies, particularly since the arrival of NASA Administrator Sean O'Keefe, a former Navy secretary. O'Keefe has made a radical change in NASA's direction since initiating Project Prometheus, which seeks to promote nuclear propulsion for deep space use.

The Pentagon's interest had cooled considerably in NASA since the Challenger disaster, making the Columbia disaster of February 2003 a personal tragedy, but a strategic non-event for military planners. Since the second shuttle accident, NASA has been reconsidering its Orbital Space Plane program to emphasize a crew rescue vehicle for the International Space Station, which could be rapidly designed and fielded. The Pentagon, largely focused on heavy lift and relatively uninterested in human-occupied spacecraft, has had its reusable-vehicle plans diverge from those of NASA.

But Prometheus could represent NASA's ace in the hole for working again with the Pentagon. Nuclear reactors are a non-starter for large satellites and possible ASAT weapons fielded by the military, since the Pentagon has not wanted to revisit the re-entry fiascos caused by Skylab and the Soviet Cosmos satellite re-entry. O'Keefe, however, has pushed for nuclear in deep space, insisting that the only way to get humans to Mars and beyond is to move to untested nuclear propulsion. He does not want to consider nuclear rockets of the type considered in Project Timberwind, but he will consider various forms of larger radio-isotope thermal generators, and small reactors using new designs.

Prometheus has been touted as the enabler of a future mission to Jupiter's icy moons, particularly to Europa, where conditions for life may exist. O'Keefe said that deep-space missions such as the European Space Agency's Rosetta, designed for solar electric-ity, have to compromise in power use for the equivalent of two 60-watt light bulbs. Prometheus would 'liberate' scientists, he claimed in an April 2003 speech, 'by moving the power available for experiments to a factor of 100 times beyond that, in even the most modest of reactor designs.'

O'Keefe said that the Jupiter destination 'is not nearly as relevant as the demonstration of the technology.' Alan Newhouse, the director of the Prometheus program, earlier gave a slightly different rationale. The purpose, he said 'is not in using nuclear power in space as an end in itself, but in gaining kilowatts of power for imaging and data transmission.' He compared current outer-planet flybys to a motorcyclist with a disposable camera getting one chance to snap a picture while driving by a target at full speed, while use of a nuclear reactor in a planetary mission would be like a bus full of tourists using video cameras as the bus lingers around one spot. The similar-ities to Teets' interest in 'persistence' for space control are more than coincidental. Prometheus is a stalking horse for future broad uses of nuclear platforms managed by the military for both earth-orbit and deep-space use. The NRO is simply letting NASA be the experimental carrier of the flag for this particular program.

While warfare in Iraq was waning in mid-2003, replaced by a seemingly endless job of nation-rebuilding, the space warriors already had set their sights on any number of targets to be potential next victims, including not only the traditional 'axis of evil' members Iran and North Korea, but even those who were partially foiling US goals in Iraq, including Syria and Turkey.

The end game was realized between the Cold War's end and the permanent war's beginning. The empire is here and now, and has assumed control. As Air Force Secretary James Roche said at the conclusion of his April 2003 speech, 'The war in space has already begun.'

10
Reclaiming Multilateralism and Peace in Space

Despite retaining a chastened sense of the possible in the aftermath of the Iraq invasion, members of the Bush administration still characterize 'multilateralism' as the willingness of allies to clean up after the messes created by US unilateralism. NATO allies and UN members may be able to provide input into creating a coherent civil society in Iraq from Shia, Sunni, and Kurd constituents, provided such a thing is possible. But no input is welcome or allowed on the subject of when and how the US seeks further unilateral action against North Korea or any other state. The empire, in short, is willing to accept tactical critiques as to how it operates, but pity the nation that challenges the validity of the empire.

The limits of the allowable are easy to discern in space policy. Japan, as a reliable US ally directly threatened by North Korea, was aided in launching its first two simple spy satellites, the Information Gathering Satellites, in late March 2003.[1] The NRO was well aware of the simple imaging nature of the satellites, and considered Japanese sources as malleable as commercial space imaging companies based in the US.

Europe's insistence on an independent navigational satellite network, Galileo, is more problematic. Even before the Defense Department began treating France and Germany as *de facto* enemies, Pentagon officials were troubled about a GPS-lookalike in which the US would have no role of denial. It is unlikely that the US will try to stop Galileo, though hurdles could be placed in the way of the European Space Agency (ESA) to indicate the degree of US displeasure. The European Commission has tried to play both sides of the street, agreeing to avoid GPS frequencies in Galileo design, while also inviting China to become a part of the Galileo coalition. The EC and the ESA also kept very clear about how much they want to avoid the US State Department's export restrictions, specifying that the Galileo system should not use US components.[2] The careful dance encountered around Galileo is representative of Europe's relationship with the US: Even the closest NATO allies (with the possible exception of Blair) want to show a certain degree of independence, but the notion of breaking off relations in order to make a clear statement in opposition to US plans for global unilateralism is simply too frightening to contemplate.

Many arms-control specialists active in space arenas know full well that the distinction between militarization and weaponization is less of a sticking point in moving to peaceful use of space, than is the failure to address US insistence on practicing space negation. Efforts to ban weapons in space cannot succeed unless a direct challenge is made to the US insistence that it can bar others from the use of space at times and locations of its choosing. To confront negation, however, is to confront unilateralism. On this front, there is little opportunity for compromise.

Official discussion on space weaponization within the UN Conference on Disarmament has been at a standstill since 1995, when China insisted on progress on space issues before it would consider limits on fissile material, while the US insisted on progress on fissile materials before it would take up space issues. Since this logjam occurred as the Space Command was drafting its *Vision for 2020*, it is unlikely that true moves forward on military space would have been considered by the US in any event.

Some so-called realists, such as John Rhinelander and James Clay Moltz, have tried to push various incremental steps and compromise efforts to prod the US toward acceptance of a ban on weapons platforms located in space. The compromises hardly are palatable, however. Moltz, for example, suggests a broad acceptance by arms-control advocates of limited boost-phase and kinetic-kill missile defense weapons. Such a position would be a non-starter for those opposition groups, such as Global Network Against Weapons and Nuclear Power in Space, which consider BMD a fundamentally aggressive weapon system that should be opposed on all fronts.

One way forward, advocated by Sarah Estabrooks of Project Ploughshares in Waterloo, Ontario, is to look at the example Canada promoted to break logjams in UN consideration of a landmine ban. Because no particular group was willing to take on the task of officially spearheading the movement, an informal

'Ottawa process' was begun, which used the power of grassroots movements and smaller governments to overcome big-power intransigence. An Ottawa effort, based in part on the principles of the Space Preservation Act promoted by US Rep. Dennis Kucinich, could make a Space Preservation Treaty a reality.[3]

Proponents should be under no illusions on the breadth their efforts must take, and the degree of opposition they will face from an entrenched US government. Nothing short of a direct challenge to US 'ownership' of space will address the attempt to weave together the current reality of BMD and intelligence, and the future sought-for reality of space weapons. Yet such a challenge will require a unified front of nations ready to challenge US power directly. Prior to the breakdown of UN discussions on Iraq in March 2003, far too many states seemed willing to entertain a 'planetary consensus' accepting a dominating American role by default. Following the Iraq debacle, particularly in light of the shoddy way allied nations were treated in the March 14–17 period preceding the first attacks, all too many nations appeared willing to take on the US directly. Yet memories are short, and it is not easy to try to pry power from the world's only remaining superpower.

Luckily, centrists within closer European allies can point to not only a broad-based unease with American power among Arab and Asian nations, but even a reticence to accept US power among traditional bases of US support, such as the nations of Latin America. Close allies of the US, such as Chile, were treated shabbily by US government officials in the lead-up to the Iraq attack, and even the conservative members of Mexico's PAN party now take a tough anti-US stance.

To move this to practical results, it would be useful to combine an Ottawa process on weapons in space, using a Kucinich-style weapons ban as a template, with the opening of a broader coalition to confront the issue of space militarization in support of unilateralism, addressing specifically the issue of space negation. The purpose of existing space-based navigation, communication, and intelligence tools to reinforce this kind of dominance, even in the absence of direct ASAT or counterspace weapons, already can be proven thanks to the brash words of the military leaders within the US who are responsible for fielding these weapons-in-all-but-name. Of course, if the Air

Force Space Command's plans to launch conventional weapons on ICBMs, and the NRO's plans to initiate Counter-Space Operations, are put on a fast track in the aftermath of Iraq, the justification for an international challenge to these plans can be made that much stronger.

A possible coalition can be seen in the suggestion by the EC to have China join the Galileo project, though this must be treated with caution. China has been a consistent critic of Space Command efforts to control space. If its manned space program, slated to put the first Chinese citizens in space before the end of 2003, follows a peaceful-purpose trajectory, China could become a useful ally of EC states. Even if China retains some military dual purposes for its space program, the capabilities and belligerent intent would have to increase a thousand-fold to even approach that of the US. But linking too closely to China in the event of such possible scenarios as a theater missile-defense TMD battle with the US in the Taiwan Straits, or *de facto* resistance by China to a possible US attack on North Korea, could create more problems than it solves. Perhaps under such scenarios, the US would force a choosing of sides in which most nations would avoid lining up with the US government any longer. But linking with an expansionist China might prove difficult, even if nations simply wanted to see the emergence of an alternative center of gravity to the current hyperpower.

For citizens of these nations, popular movements to reinvigorate the Outer Space Treaty of 1967 and demand an end to US international belligerence would indeed be useful. Demands could be similar to those addressed in the introduction of this book: acceptance of some military networks but no acceptance of pre-emptive military networks; no claims by US forces to any sole use of LEO, MEO, or GEO orbital planes; open multilateral monitoring of any military mission in space; total bans on ASAT weapons; total bans on BMD weapons; and absolute bans on weapons in space.

These demands can be linked to environmental demands to carefully monitor and limit space launches, due to the tendency of all rocket fuels to add significantly to ozone depletion. Environmentalists can be useful allies in opposing NASA's Project Prometheus, and possible future Pentagon interest in adopting deep-space reactor technology for Earth orbit. There is a potential environmental issue in ballistic missile defense, as well, even in test phases. The destruction of incoming warheads through kinetic kills, or orbital and suborbital explosions, can profoundly increase the danger of space debris, already at levels dangerous enough to have Air Force Space Command significantly expand its space surveillance program.

More needs to be done to have civil libertarians outside the US understand the links between global surveillance programs like Echelon, and the planetary dominance doctrines that feed them. Awareness of NSA global networks began with the peace-in-space community, and this community must show the new dangers represented by data mining tools, and the connection all tools have to strategies of dominance.

Of course, the traditional arms-control community must emerge from the 'conciliator' mode described by Michael Krepon in the reference cited in the Introduction.[4] Without seeking to uphold the current inequitable divide between nuclear haves and have-nots, the conciliators should not find it difficult to go beyond a tactical critique of BMD weapons. Now that the Bush administration has come out of the closet with well-defined plans for nuclear force modernization and melding of nuclear and conventional forces, the argument has gone far beyond that of nuclear stockpile stewardship. The Bush administration is in hell-bent pursuit of nuclear rearmament, and has dispensed with deterrence to such a degree that it has committed itself to endless rounds of regime change and endless preventive wars. Blanket opposition to BMD weapons thus becomes part and parcel of a larger move to restore nuclear disarmament efforts to their rightful place on a global stage.

Outside traditional legislative venues, peace activists can look to long-time advocates of peaceful uses of space who have presented positions before the UN Conference on Disarmament, such as physicist Michio Kaku, State University of New York journalism professor Karl Grossman, and Global Resource Action Center for the Environment (GRACE) Director Alice Slater.

On the international front, the participants in the Global Network Against Weapons and Nuclear Power in Space have woven together information campaigns and popular coalition networks. These are particularly strong in those states belonging to the UKUSA Treaty, with the UK and Australia in particular, home to a mix of broad-based coalitions and smaller action-focused groups, coalescing on major bases like Menwith Hill, Fylingdales, and Pine Gap. The broad-based opposition to the US-led war on Iraq has allowed these groups to reach a wider constituency than possible in the past, and many citizens globally are receptive to the information on global dominance, based on the first-hand experience they have had in observing US leaders trying to prepare the world for war.

While this success has been replicated in the US to an extent never before seen in opposition to the war in Vietnam, in terms of both speed of organizing and number of people involved, the large number of citizens supporting the Iraq war after the first assaults were made, indicate the continued problems organizers will have in the US. Americans retain a good degree of operationalist thinking, which assumes that anything that works well is good. When combined with an inability to see the national leaders' intent in anything but the most positive of lights, the result can be a populace that is willing to challenge any nation to preserve current inequities in global resource control. When peace-in-space activists tried to outrage citizens in the late 1990s by using quotes from Space Command's *Vision for 2020* to show how explicitly the military leaders wanted to dominate the planet, all too often the reaction from some indicated a belief that such domination was right and proper, given that the US 'won' the Cold War.

It is not enough to demonize the members of what *Bulletin of the Atomic Scientists* calls 'Fight Club' – Rumsfeld, Cheney, Wolfowitz, Perle, Rice, Powell, Ashcroft, and of course, the president himself. Donald Rumsfeld may want to attack two other members of the axis of evil, but perhaps a quarter of all Americans would just as soon attack another five nations while we're at it. John Ashcroft may want to follow up the USA Patriot Act with new legislation to allow the stripping of citizenship from native-born citizens, but all too many Americans would go a step further by associating all dissent with treason. And of course, it does little good to point out the paucity of information proving Iraqi Ba'ath Party links with either new weapons of mass destruction or practical aid to al-Qaeda. Many Americans are sure that there must be a connection between September 11 and the current strategies of permanent war, and so will continue to posit those links in the absence of any information.

In unfriendly circumstances such as this, many centrist incrementalists in other political realms would advocate taking small steps that work as a foot in the door to allowing large steps later. The problem is, when a nation is on a straightforward path of global regime change and empire-building, few palatable compromises are possible. This unfortunately will limit practical effects of any legislative politics in the US for at least the next decade. The absence of effective anti-war messages from Democrats was an echo of the absence of any voices of conscience within mainstream parties to the shift to warfighting enacted by the NSA and the NRO in the 1990s, or to the explicit dominance doctrines promoted by the Space Command during that same period.

Unfortunately, those committed to reversing the current space dominance paradigm in US politics will have to employ blunt language of a type few supporters of dominance will want to hear. Global empire-building embodied in the Bush doctrine of pre-emptivity, is simply incompatible with the continued existence of a Democratic republic. One must choose to support continued weak attempts at democracy in the bloated American state, or sign up as a footsoldier for building empire. It is impossible to support both simultaneously.

Developing compromise positions on BMD deployment, continued retention of nuclear weapons, and continued abuse of real-time intelligence, requires that one believe in a national leadership that has the best interests of American citizens and global citizens at heart. This baseline condition clearly does not exist under the Bush administration, and only emerged on a rare occasion under the Democrats before him. If an American government committed to at least attempting multilateral arms control efforts were in power, certain incrementalist steps to better global control of weapons of mass destruction might be possible. With the current government declaring itself explicitly in favor of unilateralism and preventive war, no such compromises are possible. The only moral position to hold in such a circumstance is outright opposition to unilateralist theories of planetary dominance. The next few years will not be easy ones for the peace community.

Resources

The following is a list of useful print and online resources on some of the subject-matter presented in this book. The truncated bibliography lists primary reference sources on military space strategy, space intelligence, and space weaponization. In addition to listing the bibliographic sources in subject context, this resource list also includes secondary sources for those readers wishing to explore side topics.

AIR DEFENSE

These sources explore the early history of air defense prior to missile development, including Air Defense Command history.

'Air/Aerospace Defense Command (history of ADC),' <www.zianet.com/jpage/airforce/history/majcoms/adc.html>
James Bamford, *Body of Secrets*, NY: Doubleday, 2001
Walter Boyne, 'The Rise of Air Defense,' *Air Force* magazine, December 1999, <www.afa.org/magazine/Dec1999/1299rise.html>

ANTENNAS

There are many engineering textbooks providing basics in antenna design similar to the two sources (Rulf, Scott) listed, but the remaining references provide political or personal observations on the use of signals intelligence antenna farms such as Wullenweber/Flare-9 and Pusher systems.

381st Alumni Assocation, 'Flare-9 Page,' <www.geocities.com/aia381is/flr9.htm>
Jack Gallimore, Memoirs, <www.aipress.com/jackmem>
Benjamin Rulf and Gregory A. Robertshaw, *Understanding Antennas for Radar, Communications, and Avionics*, NY: Van Norstrand Reinhold Co., 1987
Allan W. Scott, *Understanding Microwaves*, NY: John Wiley & Sons, 1993

'Wullenweber/CDDA Antenna Homepage,' <www.mindspring. com/~cummings7/wullenweber.html>

AUSTRALIA/NEW ZEALAND/EAST TIMOR/PACIFIC ISLANDS

Sources here are specific to the political and technology struggles in the Australia and South Pacific region, in regard to military space bases.

Desmond Ball, *A Suitable Piece of Real Estate*, Sydney, Aus.: Hale & Iremonger/Allen & Unwyn, 1980

Carmel Budiardjo and Liem Soei Liang, *The War Against East Timor*, London: Zed, 1984

Andrew Clark, 'Kerr Briefed on CIA Threat to Whitlam,' *The Sunday Age*, October 15, 2000, <www.ozpeace.net/pinegap/kerrsbriefing.htm>

James Dunn, *Timor: A People Betrayed*, Milton, Queensland, Aus.: Jacarando Press, 1983

Malcolm Farnsworth, 'Whitlam Page,' <www.whitlamdismissal. com>

David Fulghum, 'Hawaii Beckons as Test Requirements Grow,' *Aviation Week & Space Technology*, March 24, 1997

Nicky Hager, *Secret Power: New Zealand's Role in the International Spy Network*, Nelson, NZ: Craig Potton Publishing, 1996

Peter Hayes, Lyuba Zarsky and Walden Bello, *American Lake: Nuclear Peril in the Pacific*, Victoria, Aus: Penguin, 1986

Giff Johnson, *Collision Course at Kwajalein*, Honolulu, HA: Pacific Concerns Resource Center, 1984

Sir John Kerr, *Matters for Judgment*, Melbourne, Aus.: MacMillan Australia, 1979

COMPUTER TECHNOLOGY

Specific resources for computer/intelligence ties.

James Bamford, *Body of Secrets* ('Brain,' pp. 578–613), NY: Doubleday, 2001

Federation of American Scientists, 'SIPRNET,' <www. fas.org/irp/program/disseminate/siprnet.htm>

MONET Consortium, 'MONET Project Introduction,' <www. bell-labs.com/project/MONET>

National Security Agency, 'Influence of U.S. Cryptologic Organizations on the Digital Computer Industry,' 1977?
'No-Mad,' 'What We Can Learn from SIPRNET,' <www.collusion.org/Article.cfm?ID=140>

INDIAN OCEAN

Sources specific to the militarization of the Indian Ocean, Horn of Africa, and Persian Gulf region.

Larry Bowman and Ian Clark, *The Indian Ocean in Global Politics*, Boulder, CO: Westview Press, 1980

Marcus Franda, *The Seychelles: Unquiet Islands*, Boulder, CO: Westview Press, 1982

K.S. Jawatkar, *Diego Garcia in International Diplomacy*, Bombay, India: Popular Prakashan Private Ltd., 1983

Robert Tholomier, *Djibouti: Pawn in the Horn of Africa*, Metuchen, NJ: Scarecrow Press, 1981

MILITARY BASES (NATO AND US), DEVELOPING NATION STRUGGLES

NATO and US global bases and their impact on developing nations.

Mehmet Ali Birand, *The Generals' Coup in Turkey: An Insider Story of 12 September 1980*, London: Brassey's Defence, 1982

Duncan Campbell, *The Unsinkable Aircraft Carrier*, London: Michael Joseph Ltd, 1984

Ivo Daalder and Michael O'Hanlon, *Winning Ugly: NATO's War to Save Kosovo*, Washington, DC: Brookings Institution Press, 2000

Tam Dalyell, *Thatcher's Torpedo*, London: Cecil Wolfe, 1983

Christopher Dickey, *With the Contras*, NY: Simon & Schuster, 1985

Chris Dobson et al., *The Falklands Conflict*, London: Coronet, 1982

David Elliott, *Thailand: Origins of Military Rule*, London: Zed, 1978

Jeffrey Ethell and Alfred Price, *Air War: South Atlantic*, NY: Macmillan, 1983

Robert Futrell and Martin Blumenson, *US Air Force in South Vietnam to 1965*, USAF Office of History, 1981

Marvin Gettleman, ed., *El Salvador in the New Cold War*, NY: Grove Press, 1981

Christopher Hitchens, *Cyprus*, London: Quartet Books, 1974

Lucille Pevsner, *Turkey's Political Crisis*, NY: Praeger Special Products, 1984

John Prados, *Presidents' Secret Wars*, NY: William Morrow, 1986

Barry Rubin, *Paved with Good Intentions: The American Experience and Iran*, NY: Penguin Books, 1981

Oudone Sananikone, *The Royal Lao Army and US Army Advice and Support*, Boulder, CO: Westview Press, 2001

Laurence Stern, *The Wrong Horse*, NY: Times Books, 1977

Charles Stevenson, *The End of Nowhere, American Policy in Laos Since 1954*, Boston: Beacon Press, 1972

Sunday Times Insight Team, *Insight on Portugal: Year of the Captains*, London: Andre Deutsch Ltd, 1975

US Congressional Research Service, *US Military Installations and Objectives in the Mediterranean*, House Committee on International Affairs, Washington, DC: US Government Printing Office, 1977

Eugene Windchy, *Tonkin Gulf*, NY: Doubleday & Co., 1971

Bob Woodward, *Veil: The Secret Wars of the CIA*, NY: Simon & Schuster, 1987

MISSILE DEFENSE

Resources span the period from early Nike systems to Bush's latest post-ABM Treaty plans. Focus largely determined by year of publication.

Robert Burns, 'GPALS: Bush's Missile Defense Proposal,' <www.infoimagination.org/election_2000/bush_action/gpals.html>

Center for Defense Information, 'Missile Defense,' <www.cdi.org>

Frances FitzGerald, *Way Out There in the Blue: Reagan, Star Wars, and the End of the Cold War*, NY: Touchstone/Simon & Schuster, 2000

Bradley Graham, *Hit to Kill: The New Battle Over Shielding America From Missile Atttack*, NY: Public Affairs/Perseus, 2001

Andrew Lichterman et al., 'Banning Ballistic Missiles, 'Western States Legal Foundation <www.wslfweb.org/space/MCRbrief.htm>

William Martell, ed., *The Technological Arsenal: Emerging Defense Capabilities*, Washington, DC: Smithsonian Institution Press, 2001

Sandia National Labs, 'Strategic Target System,' <www.sandia.gov/stars/handbook.pdf>

Col. Daniel Smith, *A Brief History of Missiles and Missile Defense (Missile Defense Issue Brief)*, Washington, DC: Center for Defense Information, 2001, <www.cdi.org/hotspots/issuebrief/ch3/index.html>

Gerard Smith, *Doubletalk: The Story of SALT 1*, Garden City, NY: Doubleday & Co., 1980

US Air Force Research Labs, 'Welcome to Starfire Optical Range,' <www.de.afrl.mil/SOR>

US Army Space and Missile Center, 'STARS Final Environmental Impact Statement,' <www.smdcen.us/pubdocs/Pages/StarsFEIS.htm>

US Army White Sands Missile Range, 'Hera Successful,' <www.wsmr.army.mil/paopage/Pages/WU%2345.html>

US Missile Defense Agency, 'Transitioning to the Post Cold War Era,' <www.defenselink.mil/specials/missiledefense/history2.html>

James Wirtz and Jeffrey Larsen, eds, *Rockets' Red Glare: Missile Defenses and the Future of World Politics*, Boulder, CO: Westview Press, 2001

NATIONAL RECONNAISSANCE OFFICE

The NRO's own Website has a useful history of Corona, as well as many other recent programs.

David Jeremiah et al., 'Defining the Future of the NRO for the 21st Century,' Chantilly, VA: National Reconnaissance Office, Aug. 26, 1996

John Kerry, Porter Goss, et al., *Report of the National Commission for the Review of the National Reconnaissance Office: NRO at the Crossroads*, Washington, DC: Government Printing Office, November 2000

National Reconnaissance Office, 'History,' 'Directors,' <www.nro.gov>

Robert Wall, 'NRO Chief Says US Needs RLV Technology Road Map,' *Aviation Week & Space Technology*, February 17, 2003, p. 33

NUCLEAR WARFARE STRATEGIES

Useful sources for understanding the transition from massive retaliation to Mutually Assured Destruction, in particular the nuances between countervalue, counterforce, and the new 'usable nuclear weapons' doctrines.

Robert C. Aldridge, *The Counterforce Syndrome*, Washington, DC: Institute for Policy Studies, 1978

Zbigniew Brzezinski, *Power and Principle*, NY: Farrar, Strauss, & Giroux, 1983

Globalsecurity.org, 'Nuclear Posture Review,' <www.globalsecurity.org/wmd/library/policy/dod/npr.htm>

Michio Kaku and Dan Axelrod, *To Win a Nuclear War*, Boston: South End Press, 1986

Fred Kaplan, *The Wizards of Armageddon*, NY: Simon & Schuster, 1985

John Prados, *The Sky Would Fall: Operation Vulture, The US Bombing Mission in Indochina, 1954*, NY: Doubleday, 1983

RADAR

Sources on radar, from steerable tracking systems to large strategic systems.

Federation of American Scientists, 'BMEWS,' <www.fas.org/spp/military/program/nssrm/initiatives/bmews.htm>

Federation of American Scientists, 'Cobra Gemini,' <www.fas.org/spp/military/program/track/cobra_gemini.htm>

E.N. Fowle et al., 'The Enigma of the AN/FPS-95 OTH Radar,' 1979, <http://users.evl.net/~vmitchel/Orfordhis.htm>

Globalsecurity.org, 'Cobra Mist,' <www.globalsecurity.org/space/systems/an-fps-95.htm>

Jack Gallimore, Memoirs, <www.aipress.com/jackmem>

Gene McManus, 'BMEWS: 510 Full Days,' <www.bwcinet.com/thule>

Karl Redmond and Thomas Smith, *Project Whirlwind*, Bedford, MA: Digital Equipment Corp. Press, 1980

Western States Legal Foundation, 'Cobra Gemini,' <www.wslfweb. org/docs/roadmap/irm/internet/survwarn/init/html/CobraGem. htm>

David F. Winkler, 'Searching the Skies – Legacy of the US Cold War Defense Radar Program,' June 1997, <www.fas.org/nuke/guide/usa/airdef/searching_the_skies.htm>

SAGE (SEMI-AUTOMATED GROUND ENVIRONMENT)

History of the unique computerized air defense system of the 1950s.

Federation of American Scientists, 'Semi-Automated Ground Environment,' <www.fas.org/nuke/guide/usa/airdef/sage.html>

IBM Military Products, 'On Guard! The Story of SAGE (QuickTime film),' 1956, <http://history.acusd.edu/gen/qt/n/1956sage.html>

Karl Redmond and Thomas Smith, *Project Whirlwind*, Bedford, MA: Digital Equipment Corp. Press, 1980

SATELLITE TECHNOLOGY

A variety of engineering and political sources on the history of satellite development. A unified source on SIGINT satellites does not exist.

William Burrows, *Deep Black: Space Espionage and National Security*, NY: Random House, 1986

Craig Covault, 'Military Satcom Relay Programs Boost Industry, Enhance Warfare,' *Aviation Week & Space Technology*, January 6, 2003, pp. 43–5

Federation of American Scientists, 'Space-Based Infrared System,' <www.fas.org/spp/military/program/warning/sbir.htm>

Gary D. Gordon and Walter L. Morgan, *Principles of Communications Satellites*, NY: John Wiley & Sons, 1993

Philip Klass, *Secret Sentries in Space*, NY: Random House, 1971

G. Maral and M. Bousquet, *Satellite Communications Systems: Systems, Techniques, and Technology* (2nd Edition), Chichester, UK: John Wiley & Sons, 1993

Jeffrey Richelson, *America's Space Sentinels: DSP Satellites and National Security*, Lawrence, KS: University Press of Kansas, 1999

Jeffrey Richelson, *American Espionage and the Soviet Target*, NY: William Morrow & Co., 1987

Jeffrey Richelson, 'The Satellite Gap,' *Bulletin of the Atomic Scientists*, Jan.–Feb. 2003, pp. 49–54

Jeffrey Richelson, *The Wizards of Langley: Inside the CIA's Directorate of Science and Technology*, Boulder, CO: Westview Press, 2001

SBIRS-Low Team, 'SBIRS-High and SBIRS-Low,' <www.sbirslowteam.com>

Philip Taubman, *Secret Empire: Eisenhower, the CIA, and America's Space Espionage*, NY: Simon & Schuster, 2003

SIGNALS INTELLIGENCE HISTORY

Spotty resources with the exception of material from Bamford, Campbell, Hager, and Richelson. Echelon Web pages, in particular, should be examined with a skeptical eye.

American Civil Liberties Union, 'Echelon Watch,' <www.aclu.org/echelonwatch/index.html>

James Bamford, *Body of Secrets*, NY: Doubleday, 2001

James Bamford, *The Puzzle Palace*, Boston, MA: Houghton-Mifflin, 1982

Duncan Campbell, *The Unsinkable Aircraft Carrier*, London: Michael Joseph Ltd, 1984

Steven Emerson, *Secret Warriors: Inside the Covert Military Operations of the Reagan Era*, NY: G.P. Putnam's Sons, 1988

Raymond Garthoff, *Détente and Confrontation: American-Soviet Relations from Nixon to Reagan*, Washington, DC: Brookings Institution Press, 1985

Nicky Hager, *Secret Power: New Zealand's Role in the International Spy Network*, Nelson, NZ: Craig Potton Publishing, 1996

Robert Lindsey, *The Falcon and the Snowman*, NY: Pocket Books, 1979

Patrick Poole, 'Echelon: America's Secret Global Surveillance Network,' <http://fly.hiwaay.net/~pspoole/echelon.html>

Thomas Powers, *The Man Who Kept the Secrets*, NY: Pocket Books, 1979

John Prados, *The Soviet Estimate: US Intelligence Analysis and Russian Military Strength*, Princeton, NJ: Princeton University Press, 1986

Jeffrey Richelson, *American Espionage and the Soviet Target*, NY: William Morrow & Co., 1987

Jeffrey Richelson, *The US Intelligence Community*, Cambridge, MA: Ballinger Publishing Co., 1985

Jeffrey Richelson and Desmond Ball, *The Ties That Bind*, Cambridge, MA: Allen & Unwyn/Unwyn-Hyman Inc., 1990

US Joint Chiefs of Staff, 'JCS TENCAP Instructions,' <www.dtic.mil/doctrine/jel/cjcsd/cjcsi/3320_04.pdf>

Loring Wirbel, 'Confronting the New Intelligence Establishment: Lessons from the Colorado Experience,' *The Workbook*, Fall 1996, pp. 102–15

Bob Woodward, *Veil: The Secret Wars of the CIA*, NY: Simon & Schuster, 1987

SPACE WARFARE, STRATEGY, AND POLITICS

A sparse resource center until the Space Command's seminal *Vision for 2020* broke the ice.

Sarah Estabrooks, 'Opposing Weapons in Space,' *Ploughshares Monitor*,<www.ploughshares.ca/CONTENT/MONITOR/mons02a.html>

Norman Friedman, *Desert Victory: The War for Kuwait*, Annapolis, MD: Naval Institute Press, 1991

Globalsecurity.org, 'TENCAP,' <www.globalsecurity.org/intell/systems/tencap.htm>

Karl Grossman and Michio Kaku, *Weapons in Space (Open Media Pamphlet Series)*, London: Seven Stories Press, 2000

David Halberstam, *War in a Time of Peace*, NY: Scribner, 2001

Michael Ignatieff, *Virtual War: Kosovo and Beyond*, NY: Metropolitan Books, 2000

David Koplow, 'CDI Fact Sheet: Legal Aspects Concerning the Militarization of Space,' Center for Defense Information, April

23, 2003 <www.cdi.org/program/document.cfm?DocumentID =911&from_page=/index.cfm>

Jack Manno, *Arming the Heavens*, NY: Dodd Mead, 1984

Tim Ripley, 'UAVs Over Kosovo: Did the Earth Move? *Defence Systems Daily*, December 1, 1999, <http://defence-data.com/ features/fpage34.htn>

Donald Rumsfeld et al., *Report of the Commission to Assess National Security Space Mangement*, Washington DC: Government Printing Office, January 11, 2001

US Air Force, 'Air Force Satellite Control Network,' <www. losangelesaf.mil/SMC/HO/smchovll.htm>

US Air Force, 'USAF Space Organizations and Programs,' <www. patrick.af.mil/heritage/Cape/Cape1/cape1-2.htm>

US Air Force Space Command, 'Strategic Master Plan FY04 and Beyond,' <www.peterson.af.mil/hqafspc/library.AFSPCPAOffice/ Final%2004%20MSP—Signed!.pdf>

US Defense Department, Office of the Secretary of Defense, 'DoD Space Technology Guide,' <www.defenselink.mil/c3i/org/c3is/ spacesys/STGMainbody.pdf>

US Space Command, *Vision for 2020*, Peterson Air Force Base, 1996

US Space Command, Director of Plans, *Long-Range Plan*, Peterson Air Force Base, 1998

Loring Wirbel, 'Space Nets Take Commanding Role,' *EE Times*, April 14, 2003, p. 1

Notes

INTRODUCTION

1. Gerard K. Smith, *Doubletalk: The Story of SALT-1*, Garden City, NY: Doubleday & Co., 1980; Kerry M. Kartchner, 'Origins of the ABM Treaty,' James Wirtz & Jeffrey Larsen, eds, *Rockets' Red Glare: Missile Defenses and the Future of World Politics*, Boulder, CO: Westview Press, 2001.
2. Office of the White House, *National Security Strategy of the United States*, Sept. 20, 2002.
3. The '2½ War' referes to US military doctrine that the US military should be capable of fighting 2½ wars simultaneously.
4. Michael Krepon, 'Dominators Rule,' *Bulletin of the Atomic Scientists*, Jan.–Feb. 2003, pp. 55–60.
5. Desmond Ball, *A Suitable Piece of Real Estate*, Sydney, Aus.: Allen & Unwyn, 1980. See also Duncan Campbell, *The Unsinkable Aircraft Carrier*, London: Michael Joseph Ltd, 1984; Nicky Hager, *Secret Power*, Nelson, NZ: Craig Potton Publishing, 1996; Jeffrey Richelson and Desmond Ball, *The Ties That Bind*, Cambridge, MA: Allen & Unwyn/Unwyn-Hyman Inc., 1990.
6. Kinetic-kill weapons are those that use kinetic energy – the simple act of slamming into another object – as the primary means by which they inflict damage.

CHAPTER 1

1. Venona was a program declassified by the NSA in the 1990s, which was a description of how Russian spy-codes of the 1930s and 1940s were broken. One-time pads are codes that are used once, then changed, according to pre-printed code books. One-time pads were very secure in implementation, but easily subject to breaking if the code book was captured, which is why they are rarely used today.
2. James Bamford, *Body of Secrets*, NY: Doubleday, 2001.
3. National Security Agency, 'Influence of U.S. Cryoptological Organizations on the Digital Computer Industry,' 1976? (Declassified 1982?), Center for National Security Studies Library.
4. For Samsun and Eisenhower, see James Fusca, 'Radar Advances May Aid ICBM Defense,' *Aviation Week & Space Technology*, Aug. 19, 1957, p. 28; and Richard Witkin, 'US Radar Station in Turkey Monitors Soviet Missile Tests,' *New York Times*, Oct. 21, 1957, p. 1. For TeBAC, see Philip Taubman, *Secret Empire: Eisenhower, The CIA, and America's Space Espionage*, NY: Simon & Schuster, 2003. For Layton visit, see Edwin Layton, 'Report of Visit to Europe and Turkey,' June 19, 1956, Washington: Carrollton Press, Declassified Documents Reference System, 1981, 62B.

CHAPTER 2

1. Philip Klass had most details except for Corona's name in his *Secret Sentries in Space*, NY: Random House, 1971. Further elucidation can be found in NRO's declassified Corona history at <www.nro.gov>.
2. Fischer, Space Symposium panel, April 10, 2003. See also Jeffrey Richelson, *America's Space Sentinels: DSP Satellites and National Security*, Lawrence, KS: University Press of Kansas, 1999 (paper 2001).
3. Charge-coupled devices (CCDs) are semiconductor devices that generate an electric charge through the photoelectric effect, collecting a charge through an array of gates, transferring the charge, and detecting the charge. This turns image collection into a pixel-based digital electronic task. CCDs are commonly used as image sensors in digital and video cameras today, but had their first use in spy satellites and ground stations.
4. Taubman, *Secret Empire*.

CHAPTER 3

1. Smith, *Doubletalk: The Story of SALT-1*.
2. Robert C. Aldridge, *The Counterforce Syndrome: A Guide to US Nuclear Weapons and Strategic Doctrine*, Washington, DC: Institute for Policy Studies, 1978.
3. Ball, *A Suitable Piece of Real Estate*.
4. See Robert Lindsey, *The Falcon and the Snowman*, NY: Pocket Books, 1980; Dennis Freney, *The CIA's Australian Connection*, Sydney: Freney Private Imprint, 1977.

CHAPTER 4

1. Frances FitzGerald, *Way Out There in the Blue: Reagan, Star Wars, and the End of the Cold War*, NY: Touchstone/Simon & Schuster, 2000, p. 251.

CHAPTER 5

1. Intelsat interception is dealt with tangentially in several articles and Web sites dealing with the Echelon program, but is addressed most directly in Nicky Hager, *Secret Power: New Zealand's Role in the International Spy Network*, Nelson, NZ: Craig Potton Publishing, 1996, pp. 165–73.
2. Comments by Susan Miller, president of Intelsat Government Solutions; Michael Butler, COO, Inmarsat Ltd.; Bretton Alexander, White House Office of Science and Technology Policy; 'Transforming Government-Industry Partnerships,' National Space Symposium, April 9, 2003.
3. Campbell maintains several critical *New Statesman* and *Guardian* articles at his Web site, <http//duncan.gn.apc.org>. Another interesting Campbell piece, 'Inside Echelon,' is at <http://www.heise.de/tp/english/inhat/te/6929/1.html>.

4. Loring Wirbel, 'Confronting the New Intelligence Establishment: Lessons from the Colorado Experience,' *The Workbook*, Fall 1996; Dina Bunn, 'The Secret of Buckley Field,' *Rocky Mountain News*, October 15, 1995, p. 1; Ian Olgierson and Aldo Svaldi, eds, 'Colorado's Stealth Economy,' *Denver Business Journal*, April 11–15, 1996 (special issue).
5. Wendy Grossman, 'Connect the Pings,' *Scientific American*, March 2003, pp. 26–8.

CHAPTER 6

1. John Pike, 'Desert Star: US Military Space Operations and Desert Shield and Desert Storm,' <http://www.fas.org/spp/military/docops/operate/ds/>.
2. FitzGerald, *Way Out There in the Blue.*
3. Norman Friedman, *Desert Victory: The War for Kuwait*, Annapolis, MD: Naval Institute Press, 1991.
4. David Halberstam, *War in a Time of Peace*, NY: Scribner, 2001.
5. USSC Director of Plans, 'Vision for 2020,' Colorado Springs, CO: USSC Peterson Air Force Base, 1996.

CHAPTER 7

1. David Fulghum, 'Hawaii Beckons as Test Requirements Grow,' *Aviation Week & Space Technology*, March 24, 1997, pp. 62–8.
2. Theodore Postol, 'The Target is Russia,' *Bulletin of the Atomic Scientists*, March–April 2000, pp. 30–5; Inge Sellevg, 'Vardo Exposed,' *BAS*, March–April 2000, pp. 26–9.
3. Bradley Graham, *Hit to Kill: The New Battle Over Shielding America from Missile Attack*, NY: Public Affairs/Perseus Books, 2001, pp. 30–51.
4. Possel's and Barker's essays are in William Martel (ed.), *The Technological Arsenal: Emerging Defense Capabilities*, Washington, DC: Smithsonian Institution Press, 2001.
5. David Jeremiah et al., 'Defining the Future of the NRO for the 21st Century,' National Reconnaissance Office, August 26, 1996.
6. Jumper speech, April 10, 2003, Broadmoor Hotel, Colorado Springs.
7. Tim Ripley, 'UAVs Over Kosovo: Did the Earth Move?,' *Defence Systems Daily* (online), December 1, 1999, <http://defence-data.com/features/fpage34.htm>.

CHAPTER 8

1. John Kerry, Porter Goss, et al., *Report of the National Commission for the Review of the National Reconnaissance Office: NRO at the Crossroads*, Washington, DC: Government Printing Office, November 2000.
2. Donald Rumsfeld et al., *Report of the Commission to Assess National Security Space Management and Organization*, Washington, DC: Government Printing Office, January 11, 2001.
3. News accounts; <http://www.uavforum.org>.

4. Stephen Biddle, 'Afghanistan and the Future of Warfare,' *Foreign Affairs*, March–April 2003, pp. 31–46.

CHAPTER 9

1. Teets, keynote speech, National Space Symposium, Colorado Springs, April 8, 2003. See also Adm. James Ellis, NSS, April 9, 2003.
2. Jeff Richelson provides a concise history of FIA and SBIRS-High development problems in his article, 'The Satellite Gap,' *Bulletin of the Atomic Scientists*, January–February 2003, pp. 49–54, though the title begs the question of whom the gap is experienced against, given that no other nation fields these types of satellites.
3. Steve Aftergood, 'FAS Secrecy News,' March 15, 2003; Website: <www.fas.org/sgp/news/secrecy/>. Virtually the same quote was used by James Roche in an April 2003 speech, saying that superiority implied that one must deny adversaries all use of space, control space utterly, and keep adversaries from learning the extent of your control.
4. Jeffrey Becker, 'A Buzz in the Air,' *Intelligence Surveillance and Reconnaissance Journal*, March–April 2003, pp. 22–4. See also Sega speeches at NSS, April 2002 and April 2003.
5. Gen. Lance Lord speech, April 8, 2003.
6. Private correspondence with Allen Thomson.
7. Jason Bates, 'NIMA Backing New Generation of Commercial Satellites,' *Space News International*, April 7, 2003, p. 12.
8. TCA information from multiple TCA architecture sessions, National Space Symposium, April 8, 2003.
9. See William Scott, 'Rapid Response' (special report), *Aviation Week & Space Technology*, April 7, 2003, pp. 66–76.

CHAPTER 10

1. Paul Kallender, 'Spy Satellite Launch Marks New Era for Japan in Space,' *Space News International*, March 31, 2003, p. 8.
2. Peter B. deSelding, 'US-Built Components Banned from Galileo Program,' *Space News International*, March 31, 2003, p. 3; deSelding, 'Europe Takes Steps to Prevent Galileo from Interfering with GPS Military Code,' *Space News International*, April 7, 2003, p. 1.
3. Sarah Estabrooks, Space Weaponization presentation, Pugwash/Scientists for Peace joint meeting, University of Toronto, March 22, 2003.
4. Krepon, 'Dominators Rule.'

Index